Rick Steves®

POCKET
MUNICH

P9-CEC-424

Rick Steves with Gene Openshaw

Contents

Introduction

Munich ("München" in German), often called Germany's most livable city, is also one of its most historic, artistic, and entertaining. It's big and growing, with a population of 1.5 million. Until 1871, it was the capital of an independent Bavaria. Its imperial palaces, jewels, and grand boulevards constantly remind visitors that Munich has long been a political and cultural powerhouse. Meanwhile, the concentration camp in nearby Dachau reminds us that eight decades ago, it provided a springboard for Nazism.

Get oriented in Munich's old center, with its colorful pedestrian zones. Immerse yourself in the city's art and history—crown jewels, Baroque theater, Wittelsbach palaces, great paintings, and beautiful parks. Spend your Munich evenings in a frothy beer hall or outdoor *Biergarten,* prying big pretzels from buxom, no-nonsense beer maids amidst an oompah, bunny-hopping, and belching Bavarian atmosphere.

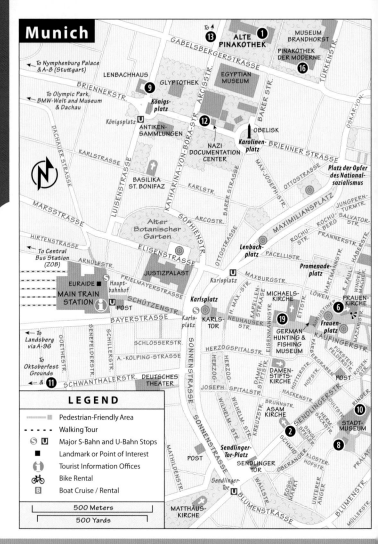

Munich

To ↑ ⑬

GABELSBERGERSTRASSE

ALTE PINAKOTHEK ❶

MUSEUM BRANDHORST

PINAKOTHEK DER MODERNE ⑯

To Nymphenburg Palace & A-8 (Stuttgart) →

LENBACHHAUS

BRIENNERSTR.

GLYPTOTHEK

EGYPTIAN MUSEUM

❾

To Olympic Park, BMW-Welt and Museum & Dachau →

Königs-platz

Königsplatz

ANTIKEN-SAMMLUNGEN

ARCISSTR.

⑫

NAZI DOCUMENTATION CENTER

OBELISK

Karolinen-platz

BRIENNER STRASSE

Platz der Opfer des National-sozialismus

DACHAUERSTRASSE

KARLSTRASSE

LUISENSTRASSE

KATHARINA-VON-BORA-STR.

BASILIKA ST. BONIFAZ

KARLSTR.

BARER STRASSE

MAX-JOSEPH-STR.

OTTOSTRASSE

MAXIMILIANSPLATZ

JUNGFERN-TURMSTR.

MARSSTRASSE

HIRTENSTRASSE

SOPHIENSTR.

ARCOSTR.

Alter Botanischer Garten

Lenbach-platz

PACELLISTR.

ROCHU-STR.

SALVATOR-STR.

PRANNERSTR.

To Central Bus Station (ZOB) →

ARNULFSTR.

ELISENSTRASSE

OTTOSTRASSE

Promenade-platz

K.-FAUL HABERSTR.

EURAIDE

MAIN TRAIN STATION ℹ️

Haupt-bahnhof Ⓤ

PRIELMAYERSTRASSE

JUSTIZPALAST

Karlsplatz

MAXBURGSTR.

LÖWEN

HARTMANNSTR.

WINDEN-MACHER

POST

SCHÜTZENSTR.

BAYERSTRASSE

Karls-platz

KARLS-TOR

NEUHAUSER STR.

MICHAELS-KIRCHE

❻

FRAUEN-KIRCHE

Frauen-platz

MAZARI-STR.

To Landsberg via A-96 →

SCHLOSSERSTR.

A.-KOLPING-STRASSE

HERZOGSPITALSTR.

GERMAN HUNTING & FISHING MUSEUM ⑲

KAUFINGERSTR.

FÜRSTEN-FELDERSTR.

To Oktoberfest Grounds ❶ 🚲

SCHWANTHALERSTR.

DEUTSCHES THEATER

HERZOG

HERZOG

DAMEN-STIFTS-KIRCHE

DAMEN-STIFTSTR.

ROTTMANN-STR.

HOFSTR.

POST

ROSEN-STR.

BARERGRABEN

GOETHESTR.

SCHILLERSTR.

SENEFELDERSTR.

JOSEPH SPITALSTR.

HACKENSTR.

SENDLINGERSTR.

HERM.-SACKS-STR.

❿

STADT-MUSEUM

MATHILDENSTR.

WILHELM-STR.

WILHELM-STR.

KREUZSTR.

BRUNNSTR.

ASAM KIRCHE

❷

SCHMID-STR.

SINGER-STR.

SPILER-STR.

❽

POST

Sendlinger-Tor-Platz

SENDLINGER TOR

OBERANGER

KLOSTER-HOFSTR.

Sendlinger-tor Ⓤ

BLUMENSTRASSE

ROSS-MARKT

UNTERER ANGER

BLUMENSTR.

MÜLLERSTR.

MATTHÄUS-KIRCHE

N 🧭

LEGEND

░░░░░ Pedestrian-Friendly Area

- - - - Walking Tour

Ⓢ Ⓤ Major S-Bahn and U-Bahn Stops

■ Landmark or Point of Interest

ℹ️ Tourist Information Offices

🚲 Bike Rental

Ⓑ Boat Cruise / Rental

500 Meters
500 Yards

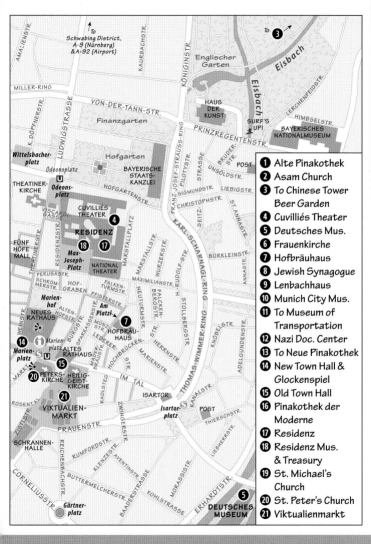

1 Alte Pinakothek
2 Asam Church
3 To Chinese Tower Beer Garden
4 Cuvilliés Theater
5 Deutsches Mus.
6 Frauenkirche
7 Hofbräuhaus
8 Jewish Synagogue
9 Lenbachhaus
10 Munich City Mus.
11 To Museum of Transportation
12 Nazi Doc. Center
13 To Neue Pinakothek
14 New Town Hall & Glockenspiel
15 Old Town Hall
16 Pinakothek der Moderne
17 Residenz
18 Residenz Mus. & Treasury
19 St. Michael's Church
20 St. Peter's Church
21 Viktualienmarkt

About This Book

With this book, I've selected only the best of Munich and nearby day trips—admittedly, a tough call. The core of the book is seven self-guided walks and tours that show off the region's greatest sights and experiences. My Munich City Walk starts at ground zero, Marienplatz, and guides you through the heart of the city, giving you a great orientation for your future sightseeing. At the Residenz, you can ogle the opulent rooms and priceless bling of the city's ruling family, the Wittelsbachs; at Nymphenburg you'll see their gardens, summer palace, and royal stables. The Museum Quarter museums take you through art history, from mummies to Monet, with a self-guided tour of the Alte Pinakothek—including Dürer's intense self-portrait and Van Gogh's *Sunflowers*. One of the most sobering and thought-provoking experiences in all Europe is a visit to the Nazi concentration camp at Dachau. In Bavaria, you can tour the fairy-tale Neuschwanstein Castle built by "Mad" (or merely inspired) King Ludwig II. And a day trip (or overnight stay) at Salzburg, including my self-guided Old Town walk, opens up a whole new world of Mozart, Alpine scenery, and *The Sound of Music*.

The rest of the book is a traveler's tool kit. You'll find plenty more about the area's attractions, from shopping to nightlife to less touristy

Key to This Book

Sights are rated:

▲▲▲ **Don't miss**

▲▲ **Try hard to see**

▲ **Worthwhile if you can make it**

No rating **Worth knowing about**

Tourist information offices are abbreviated as **TI** and bathrooms are **WCs**.

Like Europe, this book uses the **24-hour clock.** It's the same through 12:00 noon, then keep going: 13:00 (1:00 p.m.), 14:00 (2:00 p.m.), and so on. For opening times, if a sight is listed as "May-Oct daily 9:00-16:00," it's open from 9 a.m. until 4 p.m. from the first day of May until the last day of October.

sights. And there are helpful hints on saving money, avoiding crowds, getting around on public transit, finding a great meal, and much more.

If you'd like more information than this Pocket Guide offers, I've sprinkled the book liberally with web references. For general travel tips—as well as updates for this book—see www.ricksteves.com.

Munich by Neighborhood

The tourist's Munich is circled by a ring road (site of the old town wall), with the bull's-eye being the city center—Marienplatz. Ninety percent of the sights and hotels I recommend are within a 20-minute walk of Marienplatz and each other. The excellent public transportation system makes even sights outside the inner ring accessible. Despite its large population,

Daily Reminder

Munich

Sunday: The Pinakotheks cost just €1 apiece, but you'll pay extra for the usually free audioguides. The Viktualienmarkt beer garden and the crypt at St. Michael's Church are closed.

Monday: The Alte Pinakothek, Munich City Museum, Jewish History Museum, Pinakothek der Moderne, Lenbachhaus, Egyptian Museum, Museum Brandhorst, Glyptothek, and the BMW Museum are closed.

Tuesday: The Neue Pinakothek is closed. The Alte Pinakothek stays open until 20:00.

Wednesday: The Neue Pinakothek stays open until 20:00.

Thursday: The Pinakothek der Moderne stays open until 20:00.

Friday: The Asam Church doesn't open until 13:00.

Day Trips

Neuschwanstein Castle is open daily year-round but off-season stops selling tickets at 15:30. In Salzburg, the Salzburg Museum is closed Monday year-round, and the DomQuartier Museums are closed Tuesdays except July-Aug. Salzburg's farmers' market is especially lively Sat morning (market runs Mon-Sat).

Munich feels small—without skyscrapers and with streets that are friendly to pedestrians and bikers.

Think of Munich as a series of neighborhoods, cradling major landmarks.

Old Town—Inside the Ring: Marienplatz, in the middle of the ring, is a lively pedestrian zone of sights, shopping, and restaurants. Slicing west-to-east through the ring is a pedestrian-only street (Kaufingerstrasse), from the train station through Marienplatz to the Isartor (a 20-minute walk). Eight S-Bahn lines also run along this same east-west corridor. On the outer edges of the ring are four old gates: Karlstor (west), Isartor (east), Odeonsplatz (north), and Sendlinger Tor (south). North of Marienplatz, your landmark is the Residenz. South of Marienplatz are the Viktualienmarkt and some recommended hotels.

Train Station: A five-minute walk west of the ring is the main train station (Hauptbahnhof). It's a major transportation hub and home to various tourist services (TI, bike rental). Many recommended hotels and restaurants are nearby.

Museum Quarter: Several art museums (and other sights) cluster together in this otherwise empty neighborhood of broad leafy boulevards (near the Karlsplatz U-Bahn stop).

English Garden: To the northwest of the ring stretches this vast expanse of parkland and trails dotted with museums, eateries, and a beer garden.

Away from the Center: A short ride away on public transit, you'll find several major sights: the BMW complex and Dachau (north), Nymphenburg Palace (west), and the three branches of the Deutsches Museum (east, west, and north).

Day Trips: This book features two destinations—Neuschwanstein Castle and the Austrian city of Salzburg—that are each do-able as a day-trip (or overnight stay) from Munich.

Planning Your Time

The following day-plans give an idea of how much an organized, motivated, and caffeinated person can see. Munich deserves at least two full sightseeing days, and you might consider other side-trips.

Day 1: Follow my Munich City Walk for an overview, possibly stopping into some sights on the way. In the afternoon, tour the Residenz. Drink in the beer-hall culture for your evening's dinner and entertainment (at the Hofbräuhaus or a less-obvious choice).

Day 2: Tour the Dachau Concentration Camp Memorial (allow 5 hours round-trip including travel time). In the late afternoon, rent a bike to enjoy the English Garden or tour the Alte Pinakothek.

Day 3: Choose two or three of these: Nymphenburg Palace, BMW-Welt and Museum, Deutsches Museum, or more of the Museum Quarter art museums (open some evenings).

With More Time: It's an all-day time commitment to visit either Salzburg or Neuschwanstein, but well worth it. Or, spend more time in Munich—find plenty of suggestions in the More Sights in Munich chapter.

These are busy day-plans, so be sure to schedule in slack time for picnics, laundry, people-watching, leisurely dinners, concerts, shopping,

Munich and Nearby at a Glance

In Munich's Center

▲▲**Marienplatz** Main square at the heart of a lively pedestrian zone, watched over by New Town Hall (and its glockenspiel show). **Hours:** Always open. Glockenspiel jousts daily at 11:00 and 12:00, plus 17:00 May-Oct. New Town Hall tower elevator runs May-Oct daily 10:00-19:00; Nov-April Mon-Fri 10:00-17:00, closed Sat-Sun. See page 15.

▲▲**Viktualienmarkt** Munich's "small-town" open-air market, perfect for a quick snack or meal. **Hours:** Beer garden open Mon-Sat until late, closed Sun. See page 21.

▲▲**Hofbräuhaus** World-famous beer hall, worth a visit even if you're not chugging. **Hours:** Daily 9:00-23:30. See page 33.

▲▲**The Residenz** Elegant family palace of the Wittelsbachs, awash in Bavarian opulence. Complex includes the Residenz Museum (private apartments), Residenz Treasury (housing Wittelsbach family crowns and royal knickknacks), and the impressive, heavily restored Cuvilliés Theater. **Hours:** Museum and treasury—daily April-mid-Oct 9:00-18:00, mid-Oct-March 10:00-17:00; theater—April-mid-Sept Mon-Sat 14:00-18:00, Sun 9:00-18:00; mid-Sept-March Mon-Sat 14:00-17:00, Sun 10:00-17:00. See page 39.

▲▲**Alte Pinakothek** Bavaria's best painting gallery, with a wonderful collection of European masters from the 14th through the 19th century. **Hours:** Wed-Sun 10:00-18:00, Tue 10:00-20:00, closed Mon. See page 53.

▲▲**Nazi Documentation Center** Thoughtful look at Munich's role in the rise of Nazism. **Hours:** Tue-Sun 10:00-19:00, closed Mon. See page 84.

▲**Munich City Museum** The city's history in five floors. **Hours:** Tue-Sun 10:00-18:00, closed Mon. See page 82.

▲**Asam Church** Private church of the Asam brothers, dripping with Baroque. **Hours:** Sat-Thu 9:00-18:00, Fri 13:00-18:00. See page 26.

▲**Neue Pinakothek** The Alte's twin sister, with paintings from 1800 to 1920. **Hours:** Thu-Mon 10:00-18:00, Wed 10:00-20:00, closed Tue. See page 59.

▲**English Garden** The largest city park on the Continent, packed with locals, tourists, surfers, and nude sunbathers. (On a bike, I'd rate this ▲▲.) **Hours:** Always open. See page 85.

▲**Deutsches Museum** Germany's version of our Smithsonian Institution, with 10 miles of science and technology exhibits. **Hours:** Daily 9:00-17:00. See page 86.

St. Peter's Church Munich's oldest church, packed with relics. **Hours:** Church—long hours daily; spire—Mon-Fri 9:00-18:30, Sat-Sun 10:00-18:30, off-season until 17:30. See page 20.

Outside Munich's City Center

▲▲**Nymphenburg Palace** The Wittelsbachs' impressive summer palace, with a hunting lodge, coach museum, royal porcelain collection, and vast park. **Hours:** Park—daily 6:30-dusk; palace buildings—daily April-mid-Oct 9:00-18:00, mid-Oct-March 10:00-16:00. See page 63.

▲▲**Dachau Concentration Camp** Notorious Nazi camp on the outskirts of Munich, now a powerful museum and memorial. **Hours:** Daily 9:00-17:00. See page 71.

▲▲**BMW-Welt and Museum** The carmaker's futuristic museum and showroom show you BMW past, present, and future. **Hours:** BMW-Welt building daily 7:30-24:00, exhibits 9:00-18:00; museum—Tue-Sun 10:00-18:00, closed Mon. See page 88.

Day Trips

▲▲▲**Neuschwanstein Castle** Europe's most-photographed castle, nestled in a Bavarian wonderland, visitable by regular guided tours. **Hours:** Tickets sold daily April-Sept 8:00-17:30, Oct-March 9:00-15:30, guided tours depart regularly, best to reserve a week ahead in July-Aug. See page 113.

▲▲▲**Salzburg** Elegant Austrian town with a castle, cathedral, shops, restaurants, scenery, and classical music almost nightly. **Hours:** Other than the ▲▲Salzburg Museum (closed Mon) and ▲▲DomQuartier Museums (closed Tue except in July-Aug), most sights are open daily. See page 133.

and recharging your touristic batteries. Slow down and be open to unexpected experiences and the courtesy of the Bavarian people.

Quick Tips: Here are a few tips to get you started. (You'll find more information on these topics throughout the book.) Get comfortable with Munich's excellent public transportation system (and money-saving passes). Consider renting a bike (or taking a bike tour) to enjoy this green, flat, bike-friendly city. Plan well ahead for hotels if visiting during Oktoberfest (late Sept-early Oct; www.oktoberfest.eu). Take advantage of my free audio-tour versions of the Munich City Walk and Salzburg Old Town Walk. (For more details, see page 173.) If you're visiting Neuschwanstein, buying tickets online in advance is smart (especially July-Aug).

And finally, remember that although Munich's sights can be crowded and stressful, the city itself is all about gentility and grace, so...be flexible.

Have a great trip!

Munich City Walk

Munich is big and modern but, with its pedestrian-friendly historic core, it feels a lot like an easygoing Bavarian town. On this self-guided walk we'll start in the central square, see its famous glockenspiel, stroll through a thriving open-air market, and visit historic churches with lavish Baroque decor. We'll sample chocolates at a venerable deli and take a spin through the world's most famous beer hall. Allow two or three hours for this walk through a thousand years of Munich's history. Add extra time if you break from the walk to tour the museums we'll pass.

Though Munich is the modern capital of Bavaria and a major metropolis, its low-key atmosphere has led Germans to dub it *Millionendorf*—the "village of a million people."

ORIENTATION

New Town Hall: The glockenspiel performs daily at 11:00 and 12:00 all year (also at 17:00 May-Oct). The elevator to the tower is €2.50 and runs May-Oct daily 10:00-19:00; Nov-April Mon-Fri 10:00-17:00, closed Sat-Sun (elevator located under glockenspiel).

St. Peter's Church Tower Climb: €2, Mon-Fri 9:00-18:30, Sat-Sun 10:00-18:30, off-season until 17:30, last exit 30 minutes after closing.

Viktualienmarkt: Mon-Sat from morning until evening, closed Sun.

Munich City Museum: €4, Tue-Sun 10:00-18:00, closed Mon, tel. 089/2332-2370, www.stadtmuseum-online.de.

Asam Church: Free, Sat-Thu 9:00-18:00, Fri 13:00-18:00, no entry during Mass (Tue and Thu-Fri 17:00-18:00, Wed 8:30-9:30, Sun 10:00-11:00), tel. 089/2368-7989.

St. Michael's Church: Church—free to enter, Tue-Thu and Sat 8:00-19:00, Mon and Fri 10:00-19:00, Sun 7:00-22:15, later on summer evenings; crypt—€2, Mon-Fri 9:30-16:30, Sat 9:30-14:30, closed Sun; frequent concerts—check posted schedule; tel. 089/231-7060, www.st-michael-muenchen.de.

Frauenkirche: Free, Sat-Wed 7:00-19:00, Thu 7:00-20:30, Fri 7:00-18:00, towers may be closed for restoration, tel. 089/290-0820, www.muenchner-dom.de.

Dallmayr Delicatessen: Mon-Sat 9:30-19:00, closed Sun; Dienerstrasse 13-15, www.dallmayr.com.

Hofbräuhaus: Free to enter, daily 9:00-23:30, live oompah music during lunch and dinner, Platzl 9, tel. 089/290-136-100, www.hofbraeuhaus.de.

Other Eateries: Recommendations for eateries along this walk can be found on page 107.

Audio Tour: You can download this walk as a free Rick Steves audio tour; see page 173.

THE WALK BEGINS

▶ *Begin your walk at the heart of the old city, with a stroll through...*

❶ Marienplatz

Riding the escalator out of the subway into sunlit Marienplatz (mah-REE-en-platz, "Mary's Square," rated ▲▲) gives you a fine first look at the glory of Munich: great buildings, outdoor cafés, and people bustling and lingering like the birds and breeze with which they share this square.

The square is both old and new: For a thousand years, it's been the center of Munich. It was the town's marketplace and public forum, standing at a crossroads along the Salt Road, which ran between Salzburg and Augsburg.

Lining one entire side of the square is the impressive facade of the **New Town Hall** (Neues Rathaus), with its soaring 280-foot spire. The structure looks medieval, but it was actually built in the late 1800s (1867-1908). The style is "Neo"-Gothic—pointed arches over the doorways and a roofline bristling with prickly spires. The 40 statues look like medieval saints, but they're from around 1900, depicting more recent Bavarian kings and nobles. This medieval-looking style was all the rage in the 19th century as Germans were rediscovering their historical roots and uniting as a modern nation.

The New Town Hall is famous for its **glockenspiel.** A carillon in the tower chimes a tune while colorful little figurines come out on the balcony to spin and dance. The *Spiel* of the glockenspiel tells the story of a noble wedding that actually took place on the market square in 1568. You see the wedding procession and the friendly joust of knights on horseback. The duke and his bride watch the action as the groom's Bavarian family (in Bavarian white and blue) joyfully jousts with the bride's French family (in red and white). Below, the barrel-makers—famous for being the first to dance in the streets after a deadly plague lifted—do their popular jig. Finally, the solitary cock crows.

At the very top of the New Town Hall is a statue of a child with outstretched arms, dressed in monk's garb and holding a book in its left hand. This is the **Münchner Kindl,** the symbol of Munich. The town got its name from the people who first settled here: the monks *(Mönchen).* You'll spot this mini-monk all over town, on everything from the city's coat of arms to souvenir shot glasses to ad campaigns (often holding not a book, but

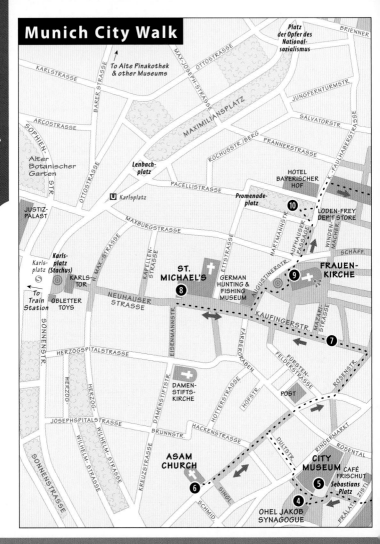

Munich City Walk

Platz der Opfer des National-sozialismus

BRIENNER

KARLSTRASSE

BÄRER STRASSE

To Alte Pinakothek & other Museums

MAX-JOSEPH-STRASSE

OTTOSTRASSE

JUNGFERNTURMSTR.

ARCOSTRASSE

MAXIMILIANSPLATZ

SALVATORSTR.

SOPHIEN- STR.

OTTOSTRASSE

Alter Botanischer Garten

Lenbach-platz

ROCHUSSTR./BERG

PRANNERSTRASSE

K. FAULHABERSTRASSE

HOTEL BAYERISCHER HOF

PACELLISTRASSE

🇺 Karlsplatz

Promenade-platz

10

JUSTIZ-PALAST

MAXBURGSTRASSE

LODEN-FREY DEP'T STORE

WINDEN- MACHER.

SCHÄFF.

Karls-platz (Stachus)

Karls-platz

KAPELLENSTRASSE

ETTSTRASSE

ST. MICHAEL'S

8

HARTMANNSTR.

AUFHAUSER PASSAGE

AUGUSTINERSTR.

9

FRAUEN-KIRCHE

KARLS-TOR

H. MAX-STRASSE

GERMAN HUNTING & FISHING MUSEUM

MAZARI STRASSE

To Train Station

OBLETTER TOYS

NEUHAUSER STRASSE

KAUFINGERSTR.

7

SONNENSTR.

EISENMANNSTR.

FÜRSTEN-FELDERSTRASSE

ROSENSTR.

HERZOGSPITALSTRASSE

FÄRBERGRABEN

DAMEN-STIFTS-KIRCHE

HÖTTERSTRASSE

HOFSTR.

POST

HERZOG-

DAMENSTIFTSTR.

JOSEPHSPITALSTRASSE

BRUNNSTR.

HACKENSTRASSE

DULTSTR.

KINDERMARKT

ROSENTAL

WILHELM- STRASSE

HERZOG-

KREUZSTRASSE

ASAM CHURCH

6

SINGL.

SCHMID

CITY MUSEUM

CAFÉ FRISCHUT

Sebastians-Platz

5

PRÄLAT.

ZIST.

SONNENSTRASSE

4

OHEL JAKOB SYNAGOGUE

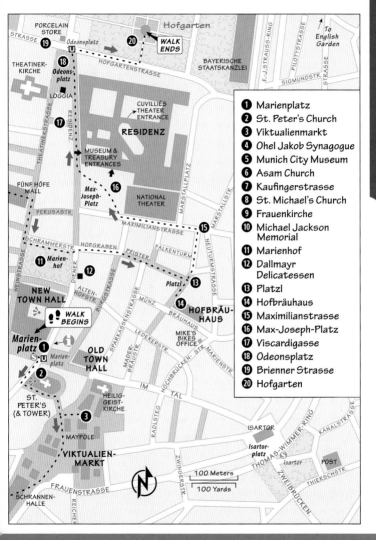

1 Marienplatz
2 St. Peter's Church
3 Viktualienmarkt
4 Ohel Jakob Synagogue
5 Munich City Museum
6 Asam Church
7 Kaufingerstrasse
8 St. Michael's Church
9 Frauenkirche
10 Michael Jackson Memorial
11 Marienhof
12 Dallmayr Delicatessen
13 Platzl
14 Hofbräuhaus
15 Maximilianstrasse
16 Max-Joseph-Platz
17 Viscardigasse
18 Odeonsplatz
19 Brienner Strasse
20 Hofgarten

The New Town Hall tower dominates—and a golden statue anchors—"Mary's Place," or Marienplatz.

maybe a beer or a smartphone). The city symbol was originally depicted as a grown man, wearing a gold-lined black cloak and red shoes. By the 19th century, artists were representing him as a young boy, then a gender-neutral child, and, more recently, a young girl. These days, a teenage girl dressed as the *Kindl* kicks off the annual Oktoberfest by leading the opening parade on horseback, and then serves as the mascot throughout the festivities.

For great **views** of the city, you can ride an elevator to the top of the New Town Hall tower.

In the center of Marienplatz, the **golden statue** at the top of the column honors the square's namesake, the Virgin Mary. Sculpted in 1590, it was a rallying point in the religious wars of the Reformation. Back then, Munich was a bastion of southern-German Catholicism against the heresies of Martin Luther to the north. Notice how, at the four corners of the statue, cherubs fight the four great biblical enemies of civilization: the dragon of war, the lion of hunger, the rooster-headed monster of plague and disease, and the serpent. The serpent represents heresy—namely, Protestants. Bavaria is still Catholic country—and Protestants weren't allowed to worship openly here until about 1800.

To the right of the New Town Hall, the gray pointy building with the green spires is the **Old Town Hall** (Altes Rathaus). On its adjoining bell tower, find the city seal. It has the Münchner Kindl (symbolizing the first monks), a castle (representing the first fortifications), and a lion (representing the first ruler—Henry the Lion, who built them).

As you look around, keep in mind that the Allies bombed Marienplatz and much of Munich during World War II. The Old Town Hall looks newer because it was completely destroyed by bombs and had to be completely rebuilt. The New Town Hall survived the bombs, and it served as the US military headquarters after the Americans occupied Munich in 1945.

Before moving on, face the New Town Hall one more time and get oriented. Straight ahead is north. To the left is the pedestrian shopping street called Kaufingerstrasse, which leads to the old gate called Karlstor, and the train station. To the right, the street leads to the Isartor gate and the Deutsches Museum. This east-west axis cuts through the historic core of Munich.

▶ *Turn around to the right to find Rindermarkt, the street leading from the southeast corner of Marienplatz. Head to St. Peter's Church, just beyond the square, with its steeple poking up above a row of buildings.*

❷ St. Peter's Church

The oldest church in town, St. Peter's stands on the hill where Munich's original monks probably settled—perhaps as far back as the ninth century (though the city marks its official birthday as 1158). Today's church (from 1368) replaced the original monastery church. St. Peter's ("Old Peter" to locals) is part of the soul of the city. A local song goes, "Munich is not Munich without St. Peter's."

Step inside. (If there's no Mass, feel free to explore.) Typical of so many Bavarian churches, it's whitewashed and light-filled, with highlights in pastel pinks and blues framed by gold curlicue. The ceiling painting opens up to the heavens, where Peter is crucified upside down.

Some photos (on a pillar near the entrance) show how St. Peter's was badly damaged in World War II—the roof caved in, and the altar was damaged. The nave is lined with bronze statues of the apostles, and the altar shows a statue of St. Peter being adored by four Church fathers. To the left of the main altar, the precious and fragile sandstone Gothic chapel altar survived the war only because it was buried in sandbags.

Find the second chapel on the left side of the nave. Now there's something you don't see every day: a skeleton in a box. As the red Latin inscription says, this is St. Munditia. In the fourth century, she was beheaded by the Romans for her Christian faith. Munich has more relics of saints than any city outside of Rome. That's because it was the Pope's Catholic bastion against the rising tide of Protestantism in northern Europe during the Reformation. In 1675, St. Munditia's remains were given to Munich by the Pope as thanks for the city's devoted service.

St. Peter's tower has great views.

Inside the church is Mundita, a saint in a box.

It's a long climb to the top of the **spire** (306 steps, no elevator)—much of it with two-way traffic on a one-lane staircase—but the view is dynamite.

▶ *Just behind and beyond (downhill from) St. Peter's, join the busy commotion of the...*

❸ Viktualienmarkt

The market is a lively world of produce stands and budget eateries. Browse your way through the stalls and pavilions, as you make your way to the market's main landmark, the blue-and-white striped maypole. Early in the morning, you can still feel small-town Munich here. Remember, Munich has been a market town since its earliest days as a stop on the salt-trade crossroads. By the 1400s, the market bustled, most likely beneath a traditional maypole, just like you see today.

Besides salt, Munich gained a reputation for beer. By the 15th century, more than 30 breweries pumped out the golden liquid, brewed by monks, who were licensed to sell it. They stored their beer in cellars under

The Viktualienmarkt sells fresh produce, gourmet foods, and beer to a people-watching crowd.

The History of Munich

Born from Salt and Beer (1100-1500): Munich began in the 12th century, when Henry the Lion (Heinrich der Löwe) established a lucrative salt trade near a monastery of "monks"—München. After Henry's death, an ambitious merchant family, the Wittelsbachs, took over. By the 1400s, Munich's maypole-studded market bustled with trade in salt and beer, the twin-domed Frauenkirche drew pilgrims, and the Wittelsbachs made their home in the Residenz. When the various regions of Bavaria united in 1506, Munich (pop. 14,000) was the natural capital.

Religious Wars, Plagues, Decline (1500-1800): While Martin Luther and the Protestant Reformation raged in northern Germany, Munich became the ultra-Catholic heart of the Counter-Reformation, decorated in the ornate Baroque and Rococo style of their Italian Catholic allies. The religious wars and periodic plagues left the city weakened. Now the Wittelsbachs took their cultural cues from more-powerful France

(Nymphenburg Palace is a mini-Versailles), England (the English Garden), and Italy (the Pitti Palace-inspired Residenz). While the rest of Europe modernized, Munich remained behind the times.

The Golden Age of Kings (1806-1886): When Napoleon invaded, the Wittelsbach dukes surrendered hospitably, and were promptly rewarded with an even grander title: King of Bavaria. Munich boomed. Maximilian I (r. 1806-1825), a.k.a. Max Joseph, rebuilt in Neoclassical style—grand columned buildings connected by broad boulevards. Ludwig I (r. 1825-1848) turned Munich into a modern railroad hub, budding industrial city, and fitting capital (pop. 90,000). But the skirt-chasing Ludwig was brought down in a sex scandal with the notorious Irish dancer Lola Montez. His son Maximilian II (r. 1848-1864) continued Ludwig's modernization program, while studiously avoiding dancers.

In 1864, 18-year-old Ludwig II (r. 1864-1886) became king. Ludwig didn't much like Munich, preferring to build castles in the Bavarian countryside. (For more on Ludwig, see page 122.)

End of the Wittelsbachs (1886-1918): When Bavaria became part of the newly united Germany, Berlin overtook Munich as Germany's power center. Turn-of-the-century Munich was culturally rich, giving birth to the abstract art of the Blue Rider group. But World War I devastated Munich. After the war, poor mobs of hungry, disillusioned, angry Münchners roamed the streets. In 1918, they drove the last Bavarian king out, ending 700 years of Wittelsbach rule.

Nazis, World War II, and Munich Bombed (1918-1945): In the power vacuum, a fringe group emerged—the Nazi party, headed by charismatic war veteran Adolf Hitler. Hitler rallied the Nazis in a Munich beer hall, leading a failed coup d'état known as the Beer Hall Putsch (1923). When the Nazis eventually took power in Berlin, they remembered their roots, dubbing Munich "Capital of the Movement." In World War II, nearly half the city was leveled by Allied air raids. The once-grand city lay in waste.

Munich Rebuilds (1945-Present): After the war, with generous American aid, Münchners rebuilt. Fortunately, they'd taken care during the early-war years to create a photographic archive of historic sights. The city faced a choice—rebuild in the old style, or go with modern skyscrapers. Munich chose to preserve the low-rise, medieval feel, but with a modern infrastructure. For the 1972 Olympic Games, they built a futuristic stadium, a sleek new subway system, and Europe's first pedestrian-only zone—Kaufingerstrasse. In 1989, when Germany reunited, Berlin once again became the country's focal point, relegating Munich to the role of sleepy Second City.

These days, Munich seems to be comfortable just being itself rather than trying to keep up with Berlin. Though rich and modern—home to BMW and Siemens, and a producer of software, books, movies, and the latest fashions—it remains safe, clean, cultured, a university town, built on a human scale, and close to the beauties of nature.

courtyards kept cool by the shade of bushy chestnut trees—a tradition Munich's breweries still stick to.

The market's centerpiece seems to be its **beer garden,** with picnic tables beneath chestnut trees. Shoppers pause here for a late-morning snack of *Weisswurst*—white sausage—served with mustard, a pretzel, and a beer. As is the tradition at all of the city's beer gardens, a few tables—those without tablecloths—are set aside for patrons who bring their own food, as long as they buy a drink.

The towering **maypole**—colorfully ornamented—is typical of Bavarian town squares. Many are painted, like this one, in Bavaria's colors, white and blue. They're decorated festively every year for the first of May. Traditionally, rival communities try to steal each other's maypole. Locals guard their new pole day and night as May Day approaches. Stolen poles are ransomed only with lots of beer for the clever thieves.

The decorations on the pole explain which merchants are doing business in the market. For Munich, that meant beer. There's a horse-drawn wagon bringing in beer barrels, the dancing beer-barrel makers (coopers), and (at the very bottom) a celebration of the *Münchner Reinheitsgebot*—the German Beer Purity Law of 1516 that stipulated that beer could only consist of three ingredients: barley, hops, and water, with no additives. (Later they realized that a fourth ingredient, yeast, is always present in fermentation.) Why was beer so treasured? Back in the Middle Ages, it was considered liquid food.

From the maypole, take in the bustling scene around you. The medieval market was completely modernized in the 1800s, and was revitalized again in the 20th century. Today, this traditional market (sitting on the city's most expensive real estate) survives thanks to a ban on fast-food chains, and city laws that favor small-time merchants with low taxes. Münchners consider the produce here to be top quality, if on the expensive side.

▶ *At the bottom end of the Viktualienmarkt, cross the street (passing the Pschorr beer hall) and continue to a modern glass-and-iron building, the* **Schrannenhalle.** *Go inside. Stroll through this high-end mall of deli shops (in a former 1800s grain hall) to the far end, where chocoholics could detour downstairs into Milka Coco World for tasty samples (and a good WC).*

When you're ready to move on, exit the Schrannenhalle midway down on the right-hand side. You'll spill out into Sebastiansplatz, a small

The market's maypole depicts a beer wagon.

Munich's Jewish Synagogue evokes the Wailing Wall.

square lined with healthy eateries. Continue through Sebastiansplatz and veer left, where you'll see a cube-shaped building, the...

❹ Jewish Synagogue

This modern synagogue anchors a revitalized Jewish quarter. In the 1930s, about 10,000 Jews lived in Munich, and the main synagogue stood near here. Then, in 1938, Hitler demanded that the synagogue be torn down. By the end of World War II, Munich's Jewish community was gone. But thanks to Germany's acceptance of religious refugees from former Soviet states, the Jewish population has now reached its pre-war size. The new synagogue was built in 2006. There's also a kindergarten and day school, children's playground, fine kosher restaurant (at #18), and bookstore. Standing in the middle of the square, notice the low-key but efficient security.

While the synagogue is shut tight to non-worshippers, its architecture is striking from the outside. Lower stones of travertine evoke the Wailing Wall in Jerusalem, while an upper section represents the tent that held important religious wares during the 40 years of wandering through the desert. The synagogue's door features the first 10 letters of the Hebrew alphabet, symbolizing the Ten Commandments.

▶ *Behind the cube-shaped synagogue is the cube-shaped **Jewish History Museum**, with a so-so permanent collection (€6, Tue-Sun 10:00-18:00, closed Mon, tel. 089/2339-6096, www.juedisches-museum-muenchen.de).*

*Facing the synagogue is the worthwhile ❺ **Munich City Museum (Münchner Stadtmuseum)**—see page 82. The humorous Servus Heimat souvenir shop in the courtyard is worth a stop.*

Continue through the synagogue's square, past the fountain, across the street, and one block farther to the pedestrianized Sendlinger Strasse. Down the street 200 yards to the left, the fancy facade (at #62) marks the...

⑥ Asam Church (Asamkirche)

This tiny church is a slice of heaven on earth—a gooey, drippy Baroque-concentrate masterpiece by Bavaria's top two Rococonuts—the Asam brothers. Just 30 feet wide, it was built in 1740 to fit within this row of homes. Originally, it was a private chapel where these two brother-architects could show off their work (on their own land, next to their home and business headquarters—to the left), but it's now a public place of worship.

This place of worship served as a promotional brochure to woo clients, and is packed with every architectural trick in the books. Imagine approaching the church not as a worshipper, but as a shopper representing your church's building committee. First stand outside: Hmmm, the look of those foundation stones really packs a punch. And the legs hanging over

Drenched from top to bottom with curves, corkscrew columns, and cupids, the Asam Church is…awesome.

the portico...nice effect. Those starbursts on the door would be a hit back home, too.

Then step inside: We'll take a set of those over-the-top golden capitals, please. We'd also like to order the gilded garlands draping the church in jubilation, and the twin cupids capping the confessional. And how about some fancy stucco work, too? (Molded-and-painted plaster was clearly an Asam brothers specialty.) Check out the illusion of a dome on the flat ceiling—that'll save us lots of money. The yellow glass above the altar has the effect of the thin-sliced alabaster at St. Peter's in Rome, but it's within our budget! And, tapping the "marble" pilasters to determine that they are just painted fakes, we decide to take that, too. Crammed between two buildings, light inside this narrow church is limited, so there's a big, clear window in the back for maximum illumination—we'll order one to cut back on our electricity bill.

Visiting the Asam Church, you can see why the Asam brothers were so prolific and successful. Speaking of the brothers, there are black-and-white portraits of the two Asams in oval frames flanking the altar. On the way out, say good-bye to the gilded grim reaper in the narthex (left side as we're leaving) as he cuts the thread of life.

▶ *Leaving the church, look to your right, noticing the Sendlinger Tor at the end of the street—part of the fortified town wall that circled Munich in the 14th century. Then turn left and walk straight up Sendlinger Strasse. Walk toward the Münchner Kindl, still capping the spire of the New Town Hall in the distance, and then up (pedestrian-only) Rosenstrasse, until you hit Marienplatz and the big, busy...*

❼ Kaufingerstrasse

This car-free street leads you through a great shopping district, past cheap department stores, carnivals of street entertainers, and good old-fashioned slicers and dicers. As far back as the 12th century, this was the town's main commercial street. Traders from Salzburg and Augsburg would enter the town through the fortified Karlstor. This street led—past the Augustiner beer hall (opposite St. Michael's Church to this day)—right to the main square and cathedral.

Up until the 1970s, the street was jammed with car traffic. Then, for the 1972 Olympics, it was turned into one of Europe's first pedestrian zones. At first, shopkeepers were afraid that would ruin business. Now it's Munich's living room. Nearly 9,000 shoppers pass through it each hour.

Kaufingerstrasse—for shopping and window-shopping

St. Michael's—a bastion of the Jesuits

Merchants nearby are begging for their streets to become traffic-free, too. Imagine this street in your Hometown, USA.

Munich has become one of the globe's greenest cities. Skyscrapers are banished to the suburbs, and the nearby Frauenkirche is still the tallest building in the center.

▶ *Stroll a few blocks away from Marienplatz toward the Karlstor, until you arrive at the big church on the right.*

❽ St. Michael's Church

This is one of the first great Renaissance buildings north of the Alps. The ornate facade, with its sloped roofline, was inspired by the Gesù Church in Rome—home of the Jesuit order. Jesuits saw themselves as the intellectual defenders of Catholicism. St. Michael's was built in the late 1500s—at the height of the Protestant Reformation—to serve as the northern outpost of the Jesuits. Appropriately, the facade features a statue of Michael fighting a Protestant demon.

Inside, admire the ornate Baroque interior, topped with a barrel vault, the largest of its day. Stroll up the nave to the ornate pulpit, where Jesuit priests would hammer away at Reformation heresy. The church's acoustics are spectacular, and the choir—famous in Munich—sounds heavenly singing from the organ loft high in the rear.

The **crypt** (*Fürstengruft,* down the stairs by the altar) contains 40 stark, somewhat forlorn tombs of Bavaria's ruling family, the Wittelsbachs. The most ornate tomb holds the illustrious Ludwig II, known for his fairy-tale castle at Neuschwanstein. Ludwig spent his days building castles, listening to music, and dreaming about knights of old, earning him the nickname "Mad" King Ludwig. But of all the Wittelsbachs, it's his tomb that's decorated with flowers—placed here by romantics still mad about their "mad" king.

▶ *Our next stop, the Frauenkirche, is a couple hundred yards away. Backtrack a couple blocks up Kaufingerstrasse to the wild boar statue. At the boar statue, turn left on Augustinerstrasse, which leads to Munich's towering, twin-domed cathedral, the...*

❾ Frauenkirche

These twin onion domes are the symbol of the city. They're unusual in that most Gothic churches have either pointed steeples or square towers. Some say Crusaders, inspired by the Dome of the Rock in Jerusalem, brought home the idea. Or it may be that, due to money problems, the towers weren't completed until Renaissance times, when domes were popular. Whatever the reason, the Frauenkirche's domes may be the inspiration for the characteristic domed church spires that mark villages all over Bavaria.

The church was built in just 22 years, from 1466 to 1488. Note that it's made of brick, not quarried stone—easy to make locally, and cheaper and faster to build with than stone. Construction was partly funded with the sale of indulgences. It's dedicated to the Virgin—Our Lady *(Frau)*—and has been the city's cathedral since 1821.

Step inside. Just inside the entrance, on the right, are photos showing how much of the church was destroyed during World War II. The towers survived, and the rest was rebuilt essentially from scratch.

Near the entrance is a big, black, ornate, tomb-like monument honoring Ludwig IV the Bavarian (1282-1347), who was elected Holy Roman Emperor—a big deal. The Frauenkirche was built a century later with the express purpose of honoring his memory.

Nearby, a plaque (over the back pew on the left) honors one of Munich's more recent citizens. Joseph Ratzinger was born in Bavaria in 1927, became archbishop of the Frauenkirche (1977-1982), then moved to the Vatican where he later served as Pope Benedict XVI (2005-2013).

The church's stained glass is obviously modern, having replaced the original glass that was shattered in World War II. Ahead is the high altar, under a huge hanging crucifix. Find the throne—the ceremonial seat of the local bishop. Behind the altar, in the apse, are three tall windows with their original 15th-century glass. To survive the bombs of 1944, each pane had to be lovingly removed and stored safely away.

The Frauenkirche's twin onion domes are the city's most recognizable landmark.

▶ *Our next stop is at Promenadeplatz, north of here. Leaving the church, turn right and walk 50 yards, where you'll see a tiny but well-signed passageway called the Aufhauser Passage. Follow it through a modern building, where you emerge at a park called Promenadeplatz. Detour a few steps left into the park, where you'll find a colorful modern memorial.*

⑩ Michael Jackson Memorial

When Michael Jackson was in town, like many VIPs, he'd stay at the Hotel Bayerischer Hof. Fans would gather in the park waiting for him to appear at his window. He'd sometimes oblige (but his infamous baby-dangling incident happened in Berlin, not here). When he died in 2009, devotees created this memorial by taking over a statue of Renaissance composer Orlando di Lasso. They still visit daily, leave a memento, and keep it tidy.

▶ *Now backtrack and turn left, up Kardinal-Faulhaber-Strasse. At #11, turn right and enter the **Fünf Höfe Passage.** This upscale shopping mall is divided into five connecting courtyards (the "fünf Höfe"), with bubbling fountains, exotic plants, and a hanging garden.*

*Emerging on a busy pedestrian street, turn right and head down the street (noticing the Münchner Kindl again high above) to a big green square tucked behind the New Town Hall: ⑪ **Marienhof.** On the far side of Marienhof is...*

⑫ Dallmayr Delicatessen

This is the most aristocratic grocery store in all of Germany. When the king called out for dinner, he called Alois Dallmayr. The place became famous for its exotic and luxurious food items: tropical fruits, seafood, chocolates, fine wines, and coffee (there are meat and cheese counters, too). As you

Moonwalk to the Michael Jackson Memorial.

The Fünf Höfe shopping mall is a cut above.

Oktoberfest

Munich hosts the planet's biggest kegger—Oktoberfest. It's happened ever since 1810, when King Ludwig I's wedding reception was such a rousing success that they decided to do it again the next year. And the next, and the next, for over 200 years.

These days, Oktoberfest lasts for two weeks in late September and early October. It's held at a fairground south of the main train station, in a meadow known as the "Wies'n" (VEE-zen). They set up eight huge tents that can seat several thousand beer drinkers each. The festivities kick off with an opening parade. Then, for the next two weeks, it's a frenzy of drinking, dancing, music, and food. There's a huge Ferris wheel. The triple-loop roller coaster must be the wildest on earth. (Best done before the beer-drinking.) Total strangers stroll arm-in-arm down rows of picnic tables, while buxom beer maids pull mustard packs from their cleavage. It's a carnival of beer, pretzels, and wurst, drawing visitors from all over the globe. A million gallons of beer later, they roast the last ox.

enter, read the black plaque with the royal seal by the door: *Königlich Bayerischer...*("Deliverer for the King of Bavaria and his Court"). It's still the choice of Munich's old rich. Today, it's most famous for its sweets, chocolates, and coffee—dispensed from fine hand-painted Nymphenburg porcelain jugs. Classy but pricey cafés serve light meals on the ground floor and first floor (see listing on page 109).

▶ *Leaving Dallmayr, turn right and right again, heading down Hofgraben (which becomes Pfisterstrasse). Go three blocks, going gently downhill to Platzl—"small square." (If you get turned around, just ask any local to point you toward the Hofbräuhaus.)*

⑬ Platzl

As you stand here—admiring classic facades in the heart of medieval Munich—recall that everything around you was flattened in World War II. Here on Platzl, the reconstruction took nearly 50 years—removing the debris, redoing the roofs and exterior, then refurbishing the interiors. Today, the rebuilt Platzl sports new—but old-looking—facades.

Officials estimate that hundreds of unexploded bombs still lie buried under Munich. As recently as 2012, they found a 550-pound bomb just north of the city center. They had to evacuate the neighborhood and detonate the bomb, which created a huge fireball—a stark reminder of Munich's scary past.

Today's Platzl hosts a lively mix of places to eat and drink, from Starbucks to top-end restaurants to the local favorite for ice cream—Schuhbecks Eis.

▶ *At the bottom of the square (#9), you can experience the venerable...*

⑭ Hofbräuhaus

The world's most famous beer hall is a trip. Whether or not you stay for a beer or bite to eat, it's a great experience just to walk through the place in all its rowdy glory.

Before going in, check out the huge arches at the entrance and the crown logo. The original brewery was built here in 1583. As the crown suggests, it was the Wittelsbachs' personal brewery, to make the "court brew" *(Hof Brau)*. In 1880, the brewery moved out, and this 5,000-seat food-and-beer palace was built in its place. After being bombed in World War II, the Hofbräuhaus was one of the first places to be rebuilt (German priorities).

Now, take a deep breath and go on in. Don't be shy. Everyone's

The Hofbräuhaus—a Munich tradition since 1880

Music plays every day at the Hofbräuhaus.

drunk anyway. The atmosphere is thick with the sounds of oompah music. You'll see locals stuffed into lederhosen and dirndls, big tour groups singing "Country Roads," giant gingerbread cookies that sport romantic messages, and kiosks selling postcards of the beer-drinking popes. You'll see tables with *Stammtisch* signs, meaning they're reserved for regulars, and their racks of old beer steins made of pottery and pewter. A slogan on the ceiling above the band reads, *Durst ist schlimmer als Heimweh*—"Thirst is worse than homesickness."

Check out the various seating areas—the rowdy beer hall and the quieter courtyard. Upstairs (find the staircase next to the main entrance), there's a big folk-show hall on the top floor. There, at the far end of the hall, is a small (free) Hofbräuhaus museum.

▶ *Leaving the Hofbräuhaus, turn right and walk two blocks, then turn left when you reach the street called...*

⓯ Maximilianstrasse

This broad east-west boulevard, lined with grand buildings and exclusive shops, introduces us to Munich's golden age of the 1800s. Three important kings (Max Joseph, Ludwig I, and Ludwig II) transformed Munich from a cluster of medieval lanes to a modern city of spacious squares, Neoclassical monuments, and wide boulevards. At the east end of this boulevard is the palatial home of the Bavarian parliament.

Maximilianstrasse was purpose-built for shopping. And to this day, it has Munich's most exclusive shops. Many shoppers are wealthy visitors from the Middle East, who come here for medical treatment or just vacation.

▶ *Maximilianstrasse leads to a big square—Max-Joseph-Platz.*

⓰ Max-Joseph-Platz

The square is fronted by two big buildings: the National Theater (with its columns) and the Residenz (with its intimidating stone facade).

The **Residenz,** the former "residence" of the royal Wittelsbach family, started as a crude castle (c. 1385). Over the centuries, it evolved into one of Europe's most opulent palaces. The facade takes its cue from Pitti Palace in Florence. Today, you can visit the Residenz for its lavish Rococo interior, its crown jewels, and exquisite Cuvilliés Theater (all described in the ✪ Residenz Tour chapter).

The centerpiece of the square is a grand **statue of Maximilian I** —a.k.a. Max Joseph. In 1806, it was Max who saved the city by

Max Joseph welcomes you to Max-Joseph-Platz, home to the National Theater and the Residenz.

graciously surrendering to Napoleon and giving his daughter in marriage to Napoleon's stepson. Max-Joseph was a popular constitutional monarch, who emancipated Protestants and Jews and revamped the Viktualienmarkt. He also graced Munich with grand Neoclassical buildings like the **National Theater,** which celebrated Bavaria's emergence as a nation. Four of Richard Wagner's operas were first performed here. It's now where the Bavarian State Opera and the Bavarian State Orchestra perform. The Roman numerals MCMLXIII in the frieze mark the year the theater reopened after WWII bombing restoration—1963.

▶ *Leave Max-Joseph-Platz opposite where you entered, walking along- side the Residenz on Residenzstrasse for about 100 yards to the next grand square. Before you get to Odeonsplatz, pause at the first corner on the left and look down Viscardigasse at the gold-cobbled swoosh in the pavement.*

⑰ Viscardigasse

The cobbles in Viscardigasse recall one of Munich's most dramatic moments: It was 1923, and Munich was in chaos. World War I had left Germany in shambles. Angry mobs roamed the streets. Out of the fury rose a new and frightening movement—Adolf Hitler and the Nazi Party. On November 9, Hitler launched a coup, later known as the Beer Hall Putsch, to try to topple the German government. It started a few blocks from here in a beer hall (that no longer exists). Hitler and his mob of 2,000 Nazis marched up Residenzstrasse. A block ahead, where Residenzstrasse spills into Odeonsplatz, stood a hundred government police waiting for the Nazi mob. Shots were fired. Hitler was injured, and sixteen Nazis were killed, along with four policemen. The coup was put down, and Hitler was sent to a prison outside Munich. During his nine months there, he wrote down his twisted ideas in his book *Mein Kampf*.

Ten years later, when Hitler finally came to power, he made a memorial at Odeonsplatz to honor the so-called "first martyrs of the Third Reich." Germans were required to raise their arms in a *Sieg Heil* salute as they entered the square. The only way to avoid the indignity of saluting Nazism was to turn left down Viscardigasse instead. That stream of shiny cobbles marks the detour taken by those brave dissenters.

▶ *But now that Hitler's odious memorial is long gone, you can continue to...*

In 1923, Hitler launched a failed coup that drew huge crowds to Marienplatz.

⑱ Odeonsplatz

This square links Munich's illustrious past with the Munich of today. It was laid out by the Wittelsbach kings in the 1800s. They incorporated the much older (yellow) church that was already on the square, the Theatinerkirche. This church contains about half of the Wittelsbach tombs. The church's twin towers and 230-foot-high dome are classic Italian Baroque, reflecting Munich's strong Catholic bent in the 1600s.

Nearby, overlooking the square from the south, is an arcaded loggia filled with statues. In the 1800s the Wittelsbachs commissioned this Hall of Heroes to honor Bavarian generals. It was modeled after the famous Renaissance loggia in Florence.

Odeonsplatz was the centerpiece of the Wittelsbachs' grand vision to expand the metropolis. Several wide boulevards lead away from here. To the west stretches ⑲ **Brienner Strasse,** which leads (though not visible from here) to Königsplatz, the Museum Quarter, and—a few miles beyond—the Wittelsbachs' impressive summer home, Nymphenburg Palace.

Stretching to the north is Ludwigstrasse, flanked by an impressive line of uniform 60-foot-tall buildings in the Neo-Gothic style. In the far distance is the city's Triumphal Arch, capped with a figure of Bavaria, a goddess riding a lion-drawn chariot. The street is named for Ludwig I (the grandfather of "Mad" King Ludwig) who truly made Munich into a grand capital. ("I won't rest," he famously swore, "until Munich looks like Athens.") Beyond the arch—and beyond what you can see—lie the suburbs of modern Munich, including the city's modern skyscrapers, Olympic Park, and the famous BMW headquarters.

As you enjoy the busy scene on Odeonsplatz, let's bring Munich's 850-year history up to the present. Munich today, with a population of 1.5 million, is Germany's third-largest city, after Berlin and Hamburg. It's the capital of the independent-minded German state of Bavaria, and proudly waves two flags: the white-and-blue diamonds of Bavaria and the black-and-gold of the city of Munich. Munich is home to more banks and financial firms than any German city besides Frankfurt. It's a center for book publishing and hosts two TV networks. Information technology is big, as well—it's home to electronics giant Siemens and the German branch of Microsoft. And, of course, Munich is home to makers of some of the world's finest cars—BMW (for "Bayerische Motoren Werke"—Bavarian Motor Works). Yes, Munich is a major metropolis, but you'd hardly know it by walking through its pleasant streets and parks.

The Hofgarten, the former royal garden, is the gateway to the even-larger English Garden.

▶ *We'll finish our walk in the pleasant Hofgarten. Its formal gate is to your right as you're facing up Ludwigstrasse. Step through the gate and enter the...*

⑳ Hofgarten

The elegant "garden of the royal court" is a delight. Built by the Wittelsbachs as their own private backyard to the Residenz palace, it's now open to everyone. The garden's 400-year-old centerpiece is a Renaissance-style temple with great acoustics. (There's often a musician performing here for tips.) It's decorated with the same shell decor as was popular inside the Residenz.

▶ *With this city walk completed, you've seen the essential Munich. From here, you could continue northeast along the path, past a couple of impressive buildings (and a happy place where locals surf in the river), and into Munich's sprawling English Garden.*

Or you could backtrack into the Old Town or catch the U-Bahn from Odeonplatz. Or enjoy a well-earned snack at Café Luitpold (best for coffee and cake), or the elegant Spatenhaus beer hall (see page 109).

Munich Residenz Tour

For 500 years, this was the palatial "residence" and seat of power of the ruling Wittelsbach family. It began in 1385 as a crude castle with a moat around it. The main building was built from 1550 to 1650, and decorated in Rococo style during the 18th century. The final touch (under Ludwig I) was the grand south facade modeled after Florence's Pitti Palace. In March of 1944, Allied air raids left the Residenz in shambles, so much of what we see today is reconstructed (as is much of the city itself).

Today, the vast Residenz complex is divided into three sections, each with its own admission ticket: The ▲▲ **Residenz Museum** is a long hike through 90 lavishly decorated rooms. The ▲▲ **Residenz Treasury** shows off the Wittelsbach crown jewels. The **Cuvilliés Theater** is an ornate Rococo opera house. You can see the three sights individually or get a combo-ticket to see them all.

ORIENTATION

Cost: Residenz Museum-€7, Residenz Treasury-€7 (both include audio-guides), Cuvilliés Theater-€3.50; €11 combo-ticket covers museum and treasury; €13 version covers all three. I consider the Museum and Treasury to be the essential Residenz visit, with the Cuvilliés Theater as extra-credit.

Hours: Museum and treasury daily April-mid-Oct 9:00-18:00, mid-Oct-March 10:00-17:00, last entry one hour before closing. Theater April-mid-Sept Mon-Sat 14:00-18:00, Sun 9:00-18:00; mid-Sept-March Mon-Sat 14:00-17:00, Sun 10:00-17:00, last entry one hour before closing.

Residenz vs. Nymphenburg: Both Wittelsbach palaces are lavishly decorated, but the Residenz has more luxury in more rooms, while Nymphenburg is known for its garden-like setting.

Halls of the Nibelungen (Nibelungensäle): This section of the Residenz, painted with mythological scenes, is closed for restoration until 2016.

The Residenz—the "residence" of Bavaria's rulers—sports a facade inspired by the Italian Renaissance.

Information: The complex is located three blocks north of Marienplatz.
Tel. 089/290-671, www.residenz-muenchen.de.
Starring: St. George reliquary and official royal regalia in the Treasury; the
Antiquarium and the Ornate Rooms in the Residenz Museum.

THE TOUR BEGINS

There are entrances on Max-Joseph-Platz and Residenzstrasse, both of
which lead to the ticket office, gift shop, and start of the treasury and
museum tours. You can see the three sights—treasury, museum, and
theater—in any order. We'll start with the Residenz Treasury, because it's
small and easy to manage your time. Then visit the sprawling Residenz
Museum, where you can wander until you say "Enough." The extra-credit
Cuvilliés Theater doesn't take long to see and is easy to fit in before or after.

❶ Residenz Treasury (Schatzkammer)
The treasury shows off a thousand years of Wittelsbach crowns and knickknacks. You'll see the regalia used in Bavaria's coronation ceremonies, the
revered sacred objects that gave the Wittelsbachs divine legitimacy, and
miscellaneous wonders that dazzled their European relatives. It's the best
treasury in Bavaria, with fine 13th- and 14th-century crowns and delicately
carved ivory and glass. Slow down and narrow your focus in order to fully
appreciate the tiniest details.

Room 1: The oldest jewels here are 200 years older than Munich
itself. The sapphire-studded Crown of Kunigunde (on the left) is associated with the saintly Queen of Bavaria—who was crowned Holy Roman

The Crown of Henry II

St. George reliquary, made of 2,000 precious
stones

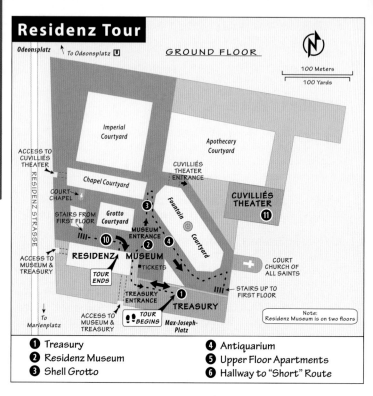

Residenz Tour

GROUND FLOOR

Odeonsplatz ↑ To Odeonsplatz Ⓤ

100 Meters
100 Yards

Imperial Courtyard

Apothecary Courtyard

ACCESS TO CUVILLIÉS THEATER

RESIDENZ STRASSE

Chapel Courtyard

CUVILLIÉS THEATER ENTRANCE

Court Chapel

Grotto Courtyard

STAIRS FROM FIRST FLOOR

CUVILLIÉS THEATER ⓫

Fountain Courtyard

❸

MUSEUM ENTRANCE

❷

❹

ACCESS TO MUSEUM & TREASURY

RESIDENZ ❿ MUSEUM

TICKETS

COURT CHURCH OF ALL SAINTS

TOUR ENDS

TREASURY ENTRANCE

STAIRS UP TO FIRST FLOOR

To Marienplatz

ACCESS TO MUSEUM & TREASURY

👣 TOUR BEGINS

❶ TREASURY

Max-Joseph-Platz

Note: Residenz Museum is on two floors

❶ Treasury
❷ Residenz Museum
❸ Shell Grotto

❹ Antiquarium
❺ Upper Floor Apartments
❻ Hallway to "Short" Route

Empress in 1014 by the pope in St. Peter's Basilica in Rome. The pearl-studded prayer book of Charles the Bald (Charlemagne's grandson) allowed the book's owner to claim royal roots dating all the way back to that first Holy Roman Emperor crowned in 800. The spiky Crown of an English Queen (a.k.a. the Palatine Crown, c. 1370) is actually England's oldest crown, brought to Munich by an English princess who married a Wittelsbach duke. The lily-shaped Crown of Henry II (c. 1270-1280) dates from Munich's roots, when the town was emerging as a regional capital.

Along the right side of the room are religious objects such as reliquaries and portable altars. The tiny mobile altar allowed a Carolingian king

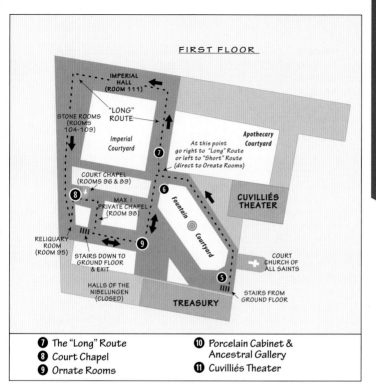

FIRST FLOOR

IMPERIAL HALL (ROOM 111)

"LONG" ROUTE

STONE ROOMS (ROOMS 104-109)

Imperial Courtyard

Apothecary Courtyard

At this point go right to "Long" Route or left to "Short" Route (direct to Ornate Rooms)

COURT CHAPEL (ROOMS 96 & 89)

MAX. I PRIVATE CHAPEL (ROOM 98)

Fountain Courtyard

CUVILLIÉS THEATER

RELIQUARY ROOM (ROOM 95)

STAIRS DOWN TO GROUND FLOOR & EXIT

COURT CHURCH OF ALL SAINTS

HALLS OF THE NIBELUNGEN (CLOSED)

TREASURY

STAIRS FROM GROUND FLOOR

7 The "Long" Route
8 Court Chapel
9 Ornate Rooms
10 Porcelain Cabinet & Ancestral Gallery
11 Cuvilliés Theater

(from Charlemagne's family of kings) to pack light in 890—and still have a little Mass while on the road.

Room 3: Study the reliquary with St. George killing the dragon—sparkling with more than 2,000 precious stones. Get up close (it's OK to walk around the rope posts)...you can almost hear the dragon hissing. A gold-armored St. George, seated atop a ruby-studded ivory horse, tramples an emerald-green dragon. The golden box below contained the supposed relics of St. George, who was the patron saint of the Wittelsbachs. If you could lift the minuscule visor, you'd see that the carved ivory face of St. George is actually the Wittelsbach Duke Wilhelm V—the great champion of the Catholic Counter-Reformation—slaying the dragon of Protestantism.

Room 4: The incredibly realistic carved ivory crucifixes by Georg Petel (1630) were inspired by his friend Peter Paul Rubens' painting (now in the Alte Pinakothek). Look at the flesh of Jesus' wrist pulling around the nails. In the center of the room is the intricate portable altarpiece (1573-74) of Duke Albrecht V, the Wittelsbach ruler who (as we'll see in the Residenz Museum) made a big mark on the Residenz.

Room 5: The freestanding glass case (#245) holds the impressive royal regalia of the 19th-century Wittelsbach kings—the crown, scepter, orb, and sword that were given to the king during the coronation ceremony. (The smaller pearl crown was for the queen.) They date from the early 1800s when Bavaria had been conquered by Napoleon. The Wittelsbachs struck a deal that allowed them to stay in power, under the elevated title of "king" (not just "duke" or "elector" or "prince-archbishop"). These objects were made in France by the same craftsmen who created Napoleon's crown. For the next century-plus, Wittelsbach kings (including Ludwig II) received these tokens of power. However, during the coronation ceremony, the crown you see was not actually placed on the king's head. It was brought in on a cushion (as it's displayed) and laid at the new monarch's feet.

Rooms 6-10: The rest of the treasury has objects that are more beautiful than historic. Admire the dinnerware made of rock crystal (Room 6), stone (Room 7), and gold and enamel (Room 8). Room 9 has a silver-gilt-and-marble replica of Trajan's Column. Finally, explore the "Exotica" of Room 10, including a green Olmec figure, knives from Turkey, and a Chinese rhino-horn bowl with a teeny-tiny Neptune inside.

▸ *From the micro-detail of the treasury, it's time to visit the expansive Residenz Museum. Cross the hall, exchange your treasury audioguide for the museum audioguide, and enter the...*

❷ Residenz Museum (Residenzmuseum)

Though called a "museum," what's really on display here are the 90 rooms of the Residenz itself: the palace's spectacular banquet and reception halls, and the Wittelsbachs' lavish private apartments. The rooms are decorated with period (but generally not original) furniture: chandeliers, canopied beds, Louis XIV-style chairs, old clocks, tapestries, and dinnerware of porcelain and silver. It's the best place to glimpse the opulent lifestyle of Bavaria's late, great royal family. (Whatever happened to the Wittelsbachs, the longest continuously ruling family in European history? They're still around, but they're no longer royalty, so most of them have real jobs now—you may well have just passed one on the street.)

The place is big. Follow the museum's prescribed route, using this section to hit the highlights, and supplementing it with the audioguide. Use my maps as a general guide and grab a free museum floor plan to help locate specific room numbers mentioned here. Be flexible. The route can vary, as rooms are occasionally closed off. Despite that, you should see most of the rooms I've described in approximately this order.

▶ *One of the first "rooms" you encounter (it's actually part of an outdoor courtyard) is the...*

❸ Shell Grotto (Room 6): This artificial grotto is made of volcanic tuff and covered completely in Bavarian freshwater shells. In its day, it was an exercise in man controlling nature—a celebration of the Renaissance humanism that flourished in the 1550s. Mercury—the pre-Christian god of trade and business—oversees the action. Check out the statue in the courtyard—in the Wittelsbachs' heyday, red wine would have flowed from the mermaid's breasts and dripped from Medusa's severed head.

The grotto courtyard is just one of 10 such courtyards in the complex. Like the rest of the palace, this courtyard and its grotto were destroyed by Allied bombs. After World War II, Germans had no money to contribute to the reconstruction—but they could gather shells. All the shells you see here were donated by small-town Bavarians, as the grotto was rebuilt according to pre-war photos.

▶ *Before moving on, note the door marked OO, leading to handy WCs. Now continue into the next room, the...*

An artificial grotto made of shells

The Antiquarium, the palace's banquet hall

4 **Antiquarium** (Room 7): This long, low, arched hall stretches 220 feet end to end. It's the oldest room in the Residenz, built around 1550. The room was, and still is, a festival banquet hall. The ruler presided from the raised dais at the near end (warmed by the fireplace). Two hundred dignitaries can dine here, surrounded by allegories of the goodness of just rule on the ceiling.

The hall is lined with busts of Roman emperors. In the mid-16th century, Europe's royal families (such as the Wittelsbachs) collected and displayed such busts, implying a connection between themselves and the enlightened ancient Roman rulers. There was such huge demand for these classical statues in the courts of Europe that many of the "ancient busts" were fakes cranked out by crooked Romans. Still, a third of the statuary you see here is original.

The small paintings around the room (which survived the WWII bombs because they were painted in arches) show 120 Bavarian villages as they looked in 1550. Even today, when a Bavarian historian wants a record of how his village once looked, he comes here. Notice the town of Dachau in 1550 (in the archway closest to the entrance door).

▶ *After pausing in the hall, keep going through a few more rooms, then up a stairway to the upper floor. Pause in the **Black Hall** (Room 13) to admire the head-spinning trompe l'oeil ceiling, which makes the nearly flat roof appear to be a much grander arched vault. From here, the prescribed route winds through a couple dozen rooms surrounding a large courtyard.*

5 **Upper Floor Apartments** (Rooms 14-45): Explore these rooms (but don't bog down here) to get your first glimpse of the Residenz Museum's forte: chandeliered rooms decorated with ceiling paintings, stucco work, tapestries, parquet floors, and period furniture. You could browse the Electoral Apartments (Rooms 22-31, to the left of the Black Hall), the long All Saints Corridor and chapel (Room 32, to the right of the Black Hall), and the Charlotte Chambers/Court-Garden Rooms.

▶ *Your visit eventually reaches a **6** hallway—Room 45—where you have a choice: to the left is the "short" route that heads directly to the stunning Ornate Rooms (described later). But we'll take the "long" route to the right (starting in Room 47) that adds a dozen-plus rooms to your visit.*

7 **The "Long" Route:** Use your Residenz-issued map to find some of the following highlights on the long route. The large **Imperial Hall** is in Room 111; the **Stone Rooms** (104-109) are so-called for their colorful marble—both real and fake. Then come several small rooms, where the centerpiece painting on the ceiling is just blank black, as no copy of the original survived World War II.

The **Reliquary Room** (Room 95) harbors a collection of gruesome Christian relics (bones, skulls, and even several mummified hands) in ornate golden cases (this and the next two chapels may be under renovation during your visit).

▶ *A few more steps brings you to the balcony of the...*

❽ Court Chapel (Rooms 96/89): Dedicated to Mary, this late-Renaissance/early-Baroque gem was the site of "Mad" King Ludwig's funeral after his mysterious murder—or suicide—in 1886. Though Ludwig II was not popular in political circles, he was beloved by his people, and his funeral drew huge crowds. About 75 years earlier, in 1810, his grandfather and namesake (Ludwig I) was married here. After the wedding ceremony, carriages rolled his guests to a rollicking reception, which turned out to be such a hit that it became an annual tradition—Oktoberfest.

A couple rooms ahead is the **Private Chapel of Maximilian I** (Room 98), one of the most precious rooms in the palace. The miniature pipe organ (from about 1600) still works. The room is sumptuous, from the

The Residenz has room after room of elaborately stuccoed, mirrored, and chandeliered wonders.

gold leaf and the fancy hinges to the miniature dome and the walls made of stucco marble. (Stucco marble is fake marble—a special mix of plaster, applied and polished. Designers liked it because it was less expensive than real marble and the color could be controlled.) Note the post-Renaissance perspective tricks decorating the walls. The case (on the right wall as you enter) supposedly contains skeletons of three babies from the Massacre of the Innocents in Bethlehem.

▶ *Whichever route you take—long or short—you'll eventually reach a set of rooms known as the...*

🄽 **Ornate Rooms** (Rooms 55-62): As the name implies, these are some of the richest rooms in the palace. The Wittelsbachs were always trying to keep up with the Habsburgs, and this long string of ceremonial rooms—used for official business—was designed to impress. The decor and furniture are Rococo—over-the-top Baroque. The family art collection, now in the Alte Pinakothek, once decorated these walls.

The rooms were designed in the 1730s by François de Cuvilliés. The Belgian-born Cuvilliés first attracted notice as the clever court dwarf for the Bavarian ruler. He was sent to Paris to study art and returned to become the court architect. Besides the Residenz, he went on to also design the Cuvilliés Theater (described later) and the Great Hall and Amalienburg at Nymphenburg Palace. Cuvilliés' style defined Bavarian Rococo, featuring incredibly intricate stucco tracery twisted into unusual shapes. The stucco work frames paintings and mirrors. His assistant in the stucco department was Johann Baptist Zimmerman, who also did the Wieskirche (in southern Bavaria, near Füssen).

Each room is unique. The **Green Gallery** (Room 58)—so-called for its green silk damask wallpaper—was the ballroom. Imagine the parties they had here—aristocrats in powdered wigs, a string quartet playing Baroque tunes, a card game going on, while everyone admired the paintings on the walls or themselves reflected in the mirrors. The **State Bedroom** (Room 60), though furnished with a canopy bed, wasn't an actual bedroom—it was just for show. Rulers invited their subjects to come at morning and evening to stand at the railing and watch their boss ceremonially rise from his slumber to symbolically start and end the working day.

Perhaps the most ornate of these Ornate Rooms is the **Cabinet of Mirrors** (Room 61) and the adjoining **Cabinet of Miniatures** (Room 62) from 1740. (Coral red was *the* most royal of colors in Germany.) Imagine visiting the duke and having him take you here to ogle miniature copies of the most famous paintings of the day, composed with one-haired brushes. In the Cabinet of Mirrors, notice the fun effect of the mirrors around you— the corner mirrors make things go forever and ever. As you glide through this section of the palace, be sure to appreciate the gilded stucco ceilings above you.

▶ *After exploring the Ornate Rooms (and the many, many other elaborate rooms here on the upper floor), find the staircase (near Room 65) that heads back downstairs. On the ground floor, you emerge in the long Ancestral Gallery (Room 4). Before walking down it, detour to the right, into Room 5.*

⑩ **Porcelain Cabinet** (Room 5) and **Ancestral Gallery** (Room 4): In the 18th century, the royal family bolstered their status with an in-house porcelain works: Nymphenburg porcelain. See how the mirrors enhance the porcelain vases, creating the effect of infinite pedestals.

The Ancestral Gallery (Room 4) displays portraits of the Wittelsbachs—a scrapbook of royal family history. All official guests had to pass through here to meet the duke...and his 100 Wittelsbach relatives. Midway down the hall, find the family tree. Opposite the tree is a portrait of the man who gave the family its regal authority: Charlemagne, the first Holy Roman Emperor. To his right is Louis IV Wittelsbach (crowned in 1328), wearing the same crown.

▶ *Your Residenz Museum tour is over. The doorway at the end of the hall leads back to the museum entrance. To visit the Cuvilliés Theater, exit the Residenz and head a half-block north on Residenzstrasse to another Residenz entrance. From there, follow signs to the Cuvilliés Theater.*

⑪ Cuvilliés Theater

In 1751, this was Germany's ultimate Rococo theater, dazzling enough to send you back to the days of divine monarchs. Mozart conducted here several times.

Your visit consists of just one small-but-plush theater hall. It's an intimate, horseshoe-shaped performance venue, seating fewer than 400. The four tiers of box seats were for the four classes of society: city burghers on bottom, royalty next up (in the most elaborate seats), and lesser courtiers in the two highest tiers. The ruler occupied the large Royal Box directly opposite the stage (i.e., over the entrance doorway). "Mad" King Ludwig II occasionally bought out the entire theater to watch performances here by himself.

The Cuvilliés Theater, paneled in carved and painted wood, still hosts performances today.

François Cuvilliés' interior is exquisite. Red, white, and gold hues dominate. Most of the decoration is painted wood, even parts that look like marble. Even the proscenium above the stage—seemingly draped with a red-velvet "curtain"—is actually made of carved wood. Also above the stage is an elaborate Wittelsbach coat of arms. The balconies seem to be supported by statues of the four seasons, and are adorned with gold garlands. Cuvilliés achieved the Rococo ideal of giving theatergoers a multimedia experience—uniting the beauty of his creation with the beautiful performance on stage. It's still a working theater.

WWII bombs completely obliterated the old Cuvilliés Theater, which originally stood at a different location a short distance from here. Fortunately, much of the carved wooden interior had been removed from the walls and stored away for safekeeping. After the war, they built this entirely new building near the ruins of the old theater and paneled it with the original décor. It's so heavily restored, you can almost smell the paint.

Museum Quarter Art Museums

Kunstareal (Art District)

Most people don't come to Munich for the art, but this cluster of block-buster galleries makes a case for the city's world-class status. Get a day pass and you could hop from museum to museum (all within a 10-minute walk of each other), browsing through 5,000 years of art history.

The Alte Pinakothek is the best of the bunch, with classic paintings by Leonardo da Vinci, Raphael, Dürer, Rubens, and Rembrandt. Continue next door at the Neue Pinakothek, starring Van Gogh's *Sunflowers*. Then browse your interests—20th-century classics like Picasso and Dali (at the Pinakothek der Moderne), the birth of abstract art (at the Lenbachhaus),

Egyptian tomb art (Egyptian Museum), Greek goddesses (Glypothek), or today's cutting edge art (Museum Brandhorst).

ORIENTATION

Planning Your Time: The average mortal should probably plan on seeing no more than two or three museums in a single three-hour visit. I'd recommend the Alte Pinakothek and Neue Pinakothek to start. Art superheroes might be able to refresh in a classy museum café, then manage one or two more.

Combo-Tickets: A €12 day pass covers the three Pinakotheks, plus the Brandhorst, on a single day. A €29 combo-ticket covers them all with no time restriction.

Getting There: Handy tram #27 whisks you right from Karlsplatz to the Pinakothek stop, with the three Pinakothek museums right there. Or take bus #100 from either the train station or Odeonsplatz. Or take the U-2 to Königsplatz, where you'll find the Lenbachhaus and Glyptothek museums, and additional museums a few blocks away.

Alte Pinakothek: €4 during renovation (otherwise €7), €1 on Sun, covered by €12 day pass, open Wed-Sun 10:00-18:00, Tue 10:00-20:00, closed Mon, last entry 30 minutes before closing, free audioguide (€4.50 on Sun), no flash photos, Barer Strasse 27, tel. 089/2380-5216, www.pinakothek.de/alte-pinakothek.

Neue Pinakothek: €7, €1 on Sun, covered by €12 day pass, open Thu-Mon 10:00-18:00, Wed 10:00-20:00, closed Tue, free audioguide (€4.50 on Sun), classy café, Barer Strasse 29 but enter on Theresienstrasse, tel. 089/2380-5195, www.pinakothek.de/neue-pinakothek.

Pinakothek der Moderne: €10, €1 on Sun, covered by €12 day pass, open Tue-Sun 10:00-18:00, Thu until 20:00, closed Mon, free audioguide (€4.50 on Sun); Barer Strasse 40, tel. 089/2380-5360, www.pinakothek.de/pinakothek-der-moderne.

Lenbachhaus: €10, includes audioguide, Tue 10:00-21:00, Wed-Sun 10:00-18:00, closed Mon, good but pricey café, tel. 089/2333-2000, www.lenbachhaus.de.

Egyptian Museum: €12, €6 on Sun, Tue 10:00-20:00, Wed-Sun 10:00-18:00, closed Mon, free audioguide, Gabelsbergerstrasse 35, tel. 089/2892-7630, www.smaek.de.

TOURING THE MUSEUMS

This chapter presents the various museums in order of how I'd rate them. Afternoon/evening is a great time to go, as most museums are open late one night of the week.

▲▲Alte Pinakothek

Bavaria's best painting gallery (the "Old Art Gallery," pronounced ALL-teh pee-nah-koh-TEHK) shows off a world-class collection of European masterpieces from the 14th to 19th century, starring the two tumultuous centuries (1450-1650) when Europe went from medieval to modern. See paintings from the Italian Renaissance (Raphael, Leonardo, Botticelli, Titian) and the German Renaissance it inspired (Albrecht Dürer). The Reformation of Martin Luther eventually split Europe into two subcultures—Protestants and Catholics—with two distinct art styles (exemplified by Rembrandt and Rubens, respectively).

Note that the musem will likely be under renovation when you visit, though you should find the majority of the rooms on this tour to be open—ask when you arrive.

▶ *All the paintings we'll see are on the upper floor, which is laid out like a barbell. This tour starts at one fat end and works its way through the*

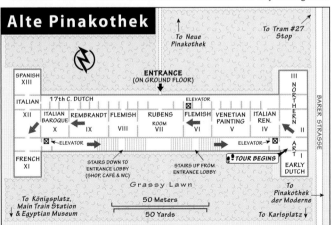

"handle" to the other end. From the ticket counter, head up the stairway to the left to reach the first rooms.

German Renaissance—Room II: Albrecht Altdorfer's *The Battle of Issus (Schlacht bei Issus)* shows a world at war. Masses of soldiers are swept along in the currents and tides of a battle completely beyond their control, their confused motion reflected in the swirling sky. We see the battle from a great height, giving us a godlike perspective. Though the painting depicts Alexander the Great's history-changing victory over the Persians (find the Persian king Darius turning and fleeing), it could as easily have been Germany in the 1520s. Christians were fighting Muslims, peasants battled masters, and Catholics and Protestants were squaring off for a century of conflict. The armies melt into a huge landscape, leaving the impression that the battle goes on forever.

Albrecht Dürer's larger-than-life *Four Apostles* (*Johannes und Petrus* and *Paulus und Marcus*) are saints of a radical new religion: Martin Luther's Protestantism. Just as Luther challenged Church authority, Dürer—a friend of Luther's—strips these saints of any rich clothes, halos, or trappings of power and gives them down-to-earth human features: receding hairlines, wrinkles, and suspicious eyes. The inscription warns German rulers to

Altdorfer shows a world at war.

Dürer's self-portrait—artist as saint

follow the Bible rather than Catholic Church leaders. The figure of Mark—a Bible in one hand and a sword in the other—is a fitting symbol of the dangerous times.

Dürer's *Self-Portrait in Fur Coat (Selbstbildnis im Pelzrock)* looks like Jesus Christ but is actually 28-year-old Dürer himself (per his inscription: "XXVIII"), gazing out, with his right hand solemnly giving a blessing. This is the ultimate image of humanism: the artist as an instrument of God's continued creation. Get close and enjoy the intricately braided hair, the skin texture, and the fur collar. To the left of the head is Dürer's famous monogram—"A.D." in the form of a pyramid.

Italian Renaissance—Room IV: With the Italian Renaissance—the "rebirth" of interest in the art and learning of ancient Greece and Rome—artists captured the realism, three-dimensionality, and symmetry found in classical statues. Twenty-one-year-old Leonardo da Vinci's *Virgin and Child (Maria mit dem Kinde)* need no halos—they radiate purity. Mary is a solid pyramid of maternal love, flanked by Renaissance-arch windows that look out on the hazy distance. Baby Jesus reaches out to play innocently with a carnation, the blood-colored symbol of his eventual death.

Raphael's *Holy Family at the Canigiani House (Die hl. Familie aus dem Hause Canigiani)* takes Leonardo's pyramid form and runs with it. Father Joseph forms the peak, with his staff as the strong central axis. Mary and Jesus (on the right) form a pyramid-within-the-pyramid, as do Elizabeth and baby John the Baptist on the left. They all exchange meaningful eye contact, safe within the bounds of the stable family structure.

In Botticelli's *Lamentation over Christ (Die Beweinung Christi),* the Renaissance "pyramid" implodes, as the weight of the dead Christ drags everyone down, and the tomb grins darkly behind them.

Venetian Painting—Room V: In Titian's *Christ Crowned with Thorns (Die Dornenkrönung),* a powerfully built Christ sits silently enduring torture by prison guards. The painting is by Venice's greatest Renaissance painter, but there's no symmetry, no pyramid form, and the brushwork is intentionally messy and Impressionistic. By the way, this is the first painting we've seen done on canvas rather than wood, as artists experimented with vegetable oil-based paints.

Rubens and Baroque—Room VII: Europe's religious wars split the Continent in two—Protestants in the northern countries, Catholics in the south. (Germany itself was divided, with Bavaria remaining Catholic.) The Baroque style, popular in Catholic countries, featured large canvases,

This rare, early Leonardo da Vinci has the artist's trademark pyramid composition and fantasy landscape.

bright colors, lots of flesh, rippling motion, wild emotions, grand themes... and pudgy winged babies, the sure sign of Baroque. This room holds several canvases by the great Flemish painter Peter Paul Rubens.

In Rubens' 300-square-foot *Great Last Judgment (Das Grosse Jüngste Gericht),* Christ raises the righteous up to heaven (left side) and damns the sinners to hell (on the right). This swirling cycle of nudes was considered risqué and kept under wraps by the very monks who'd commissioned it.

Rubens and Isabella Brant shows the artist with his first wife, both of them the very picture of health, wealth, and success. They lean together unconsciously, as people in love will do, with their hands clasped in mutual affection. When his first wife died, 53-year-old Rubens found a replacement—16-year-old Hélène Fourment, shown in an adjacent painting (just to the left) in her wedding dress. You may recognize Hélène's face in other Rubens paintings.

The Rape of the Daughters of Leucippus (Der Raub der Töchter des Leukippos) has many of Rubens' most typical elements—fleshy, emotional, rippling motion; bright colors; and a classical subject. The legendary twins Castor and Pollux crash a wedding and steal the brides as their own.

Titian signals the end of the Renaissance.

Rubens and his first wife, Isabella

Rubens specialized in tourist-dwarfing canvases populated with twisting nudes in complex compositions.

The chaos of flailing limbs and rearing horses is all held together in a subtle X-shaped composition. Like the weaving counterpoint in a Baroque fugue, Rubens balances opposites.

Notice that Rubens' canvases were—to a great extent—cranked out by his students and assistants from small "cartoons" the master himself made (displayed in the side room).

Rembrandt and Dutch—Room IX: From Holland, Rembrandt van Rijn's *Six Paintings from the Life of Christ* are a down-to-earth look at supernatural events. The *Adoration (Die Anbetung der Hirten)* of Baby Jesus takes place in a 17th-century Dutch barn with ordinary folk as models. The canvases are dark brown, lit by strong light. The *Adoration*'s light source is the Baby Jesus himself—literally the "light of the world." In the *Deposition (Kreuzabnahme),* the light bounces off Christ's pale body onto his mother Mary, who has fainted in the shadows, showing how his death also hurts her. The drama is underplayed, with subdued emotions. In the *Raising of the Cross (Kreuzaufrichtung),* a man dressed in blue is looking on—a self-portrait of Rembrandt.

▲Neue Pinakothek

The Alte Pinakothek's younger sister is an easy-to-like collection located just across the street, showing paintings from 1800 to 1920. Breeze through a smattering of Romantics on your way to the museum's highlight: some world-class Impressionist paintings, and one of Van Gogh's *Sunflowers.*

▶ *Pick up the audioguide and floor plan, and follow their prescribed route. Along the way, be sure to hit these highlights.*

Rooms 1-3: In Room 1, Jacques-Louis David's curly-haired *Comtesse de Sorcy* shows the French noblewoman dressed in the ancient-Greek-style fashions popular during the Revolution. Room 3 features English painters—Turner's stormy seascapes and Gainsborough's contemplative *Mrs. Thomas Hibbert.* Nearby, you'll see other less-famous works by other major European artists.

Rooms 4-18: These rooms—the bulk of the museum—feature colorful, pretty, realistic (and mostly forgettable) paintings by German Romantics. In the remarkable *King Ludwig I in Coronation Robes* (Room 8), the young playboy king is both regal and rakish. (For more on the king, the artist, and their Gallery of Beauties, see page 67.) Caspar David Friedrich (Room 9) is Germany's best-known chronicler of the awe-inspiring power of nature (though these small canvases aren't his best). Carl Spitzweg's tiny *The Poor Poet* (Room 10a) is often reproduced. Room 13 has huge (hard-to-miss) canvases: *The Destruction of Jerusalem by Titus,* and the nationalist-themed *Thusnelda Led in Germanicus' Triumph,* showing a German noblewoman and her son, captured by the Romans, being paraded before the emperor.

Rooms 19-22: In these rooms, you'll find classic examples from all

Ludwig I collected art—and mistresses.

Van Gogh and Impressionists at the "Neue"

of the Impressionist and Post-Impressionist masters: Degas' snapshots of women at work, Monet's sunny landscapes and water lilies, Manet's bourgeois Realism, Cézanne's still lifes, and Gauguin's languid Tahitian ladies. Van Gogh's *Sunflowers* is one of eleven similar canvases, which he used to decorate his home in Arles when Gauguin came to visit. In the final rooms, see works by Gustav Klimt and Munich's answer to Klimt, Franz von Stuck. The Neue Pinakothek may whet your appetite for even *neuer* art, found nearby at the Pinakothek der Moderne, Lenbachhaus, and the Museum Brandhorst.

▲Pinakothek der Moderne

This museum picks up where the other two Pinakotheks leave off, covering the 20th century. Most of the building houses temporary exhibits and constantly rotating collections, but there are two (fairly) permanent exhibits, with excellent English descriptions throughout. The striking, white, high-ceilinged building itself is also worth a look—it's free to step into the atrium.

The manageably sized **Classical Modernism wing** covers many of the stars of modern art—Picasso, Dalí, Miró, and so on. The museum's strength is the German contribution. The Expressionists rendered reality in deep colors and bold black outlines. Munich's Blue Rider Group (Kandinsky, Klee, Marc) took it the next step, by abandoning reality altogether and expressing themselves with only color and line. One or two rooms display "degenerate art"—paintings confiscated by the Nazis and eventually rescued by an art lover. Max Beckmann (whose work is usually in Room 9) witnessed the rise of Nazism—and was branded a degenerate—and his symbol-laced works chronicle the cynicism of the time.

The **design wing** is easy to appreciate. From chairs to bikes to

The Pinakothek der Moderne has Kandinsky... ... as does the underrated Lenbachhaus.

blenders to cars and computers, these are everyday objects that work efficiently but also have a sleek artistic flair.

Lenbachhaus

Little ol' Munich blew the art world's mind when a posse of rebellious art-school cronies formed the revolutionary "Blue Rider" *(Blaue Reiter)* group and galloped toward a brand new horizon—abstract art. In the Lenbachhaus' pleasant galleries you can witness the birth of Modernist non-representational art, with paintings by Kandinsky, Klee, and Marc. Then stroll the rest of the building's offerings, including the apartments of painter Franz von Lenbach, whose original villa and studio are now largely enclosed by the modern museum building.

▶ *The revolution begins on the second floor, with seemingly innocuous paintings of the cute Bavarian town of Murnau.*

Origins of the Blue Rider Group: It was here in 1908 that two Munich couples—Wassily Kandinsky, Alexej Jawlensky, and their artist girl-friends—came for vacation. The four painted together—it's hard to tell their work apart—employing intense colors, thick paint, and bold black outlines. Over the next few years (c. 1911-1914), they'd gather a group of Munich-based artists calling themselves the Blue Rider (the origin of the name is debated), which included Paul Klee and Franz Marc. They were all devoted to expressing the spiritual truths they felt within by using intense colors and geometric shapes.

The Blue Rider might have remained a minor offshoot of German Expressionism, but, as the next rooms show, its members went on to great-er things, pioneering abstract art. As they focused on the spiritual, they paid less attention to recreating the physical world realistically on canvas and more attention to the colors and lines alone. Kandinsky's "Improvisations"—like a jazz musician improvising a new pattern of notes from a set scale—eventually became the art world's first purely abstract canvases. Soon Kandinsky was teaching at the famous Bauhaus school in Weimar, and his style spread everywhere. Jawlensky and Klee also went on to a simpler and more abstract style. Between the second-floor Blue Rider rooms is one section ("New Objectivity") with German art from the interwar years.

▶ *One floor down is the "Art After 1945" section.*

Art After 1945: You'll see big, empty canvases by the Abstract Expressionists who—like Kandinsky and his Blue Rider contemporaries—tried to "express" deep truths through "abstract" color and line alone. You'll see other recent pieces, most of them provocative. This floor also has a section devoted to several oddball installations by Joseph Beuys. (Is that art, or did the janitor just leave a broom here?) The far wing's stash of 19th-century paintings (on both floors) provides a nice contrast to all the abstract stuff (but skip it if you're also hitting the Neue Pinakothek, which has a better collection of similar works). Finally, across the entry hall from the ticket desk and up one floor, check out portraits of 19th-century notables by the painter who lived and worked here in what is now the museum that bears his name, Franz von Lenbach.

More Museums

To enjoy the ▲ **Egyptian Museum** you don't need a strong interest in ancient Egypt. With its smart design and touch-screen terminals, you feel like you're entering an ancient tomb with beautifully lit art. The **Museum Brandhorst** covers late-20th-century art (Andy Warhol, Cy Twombly), contained in a colorful building (closed Mon, www.museum-brandhorst. de). The **Glyptothek** is an impressive collection of Greek and Roman sculpture (closed Mon, www.antike-am-koenigsplatz.mwn.de/glyptothek). The **Nazi Documentation Center** is also in this quarter—for details see page 84.

Nymphenburg Palace Tour

For 200 years, this oasis of palaces and gardens was the Wittelsbach rulers' summer vacation home, a getaway from the sniping politics of court life in the city. Their kids could play, picnic, ride horses, and frolic in the ponds and gardens, while the adults played cards, listened to music, and sipped coffee on the veranda. It was at Nymphenburg that a seven-year-old Mozart gave a widely heralded concert, that 60-year-old Ludwig I courted the femme fatale Lola Montez, and that "Mad" King Ludwig II (Ludwig I's grandson) was born and baptized.

Today, Nymphenburg Palace and the surrounding one-square-mile park are great for a royal stroll or discreet picnic (see map on page 65).

You can tour the Bavarian royal family's summer quarters, visit the Royal Stables Museum (carriages, sleighs, and porcelain), and browse a few mini-palaces on the grounds. Allow at least three hours (including travel time) to see the palace complex at a leisurely pace.

ORIENTATION

Cost: Palace-€6; Royal Stables Museum-€4.50; €11.50 combo-ticket (€8.50 off-season) covers the palace, Royal Stables Museum, and outlying sights open in summer.

Hours: All of these sights are open daily April-mid-Oct 9:00-18:00, mid-Oct-March 10:00-16:00—except for Amalienburg and the other small palaces in the park, which are closed mid-Oct-March. The park is open daily 6:30-dusk and free to enter.

Information: The place is stingy on free information. The €3.50 audio-guide (covering only the main palace) is serviceable. Tel. 089/179-080, www.schloss-nymphenburg.de.

Getting There: The palace is three miles northwest of central Munich. Take tram #17 (direction: Amalienburgstrasse) from the north side of the train station (or catch it at Karlsplatz). In 15 minutes you reach the Schloss Nymphenburg stop. From the bridge by the tram stop, you'll see the palace—a 10-minute walk away. By bike, the palace is a pleasant 30-minute ride from the main train station, following Arnulfstrasse. Biking in the palace grounds is not permitted.

Eating: A café serves lunches in the former palm house, behind and to the right of the palace (open year-round). More eating options are near the tram stop, including a bakery with sandwiches.

Grand entrance to Nymphenburg Palace

Ludwig I and his "girls"

THE TOUR BEGINS

Nymphenburg Palace

In 1662, after 10 years of trying, the Bavarian ruler Ferdinand Maria and his wife, Henriette Adelaide of Savoy, finally had a son, Max Emanuel. In gratitude for a male heir, Ferdinand gave this land to his Italian wife, who proceeded to build an Italian-style Baroque palace. Their son expanded the palace to today's size. (Today's Wittelsbachs, who still refer to themselves as "princes" or "dukes," live in one wing of the palace.)

▶ Start your visit by touring the 16 rooms of the main palace. After buying your ticket, you go upstairs, where you enter into the...

Great Hall (a.k.a. Stone Hall)

As the central room of the palace, this light and airy space was the dining

hall, site of big Wittelsbach family festivals. One of the grandest and best-preserved Rococo rooms in Bavaria (from about 1760), it sports elaborate stucco work by François de Cuvilliés (of Residenz fame) and a ceiling fresco by Johann Baptist Zimmermann (of Wieskirche fame).

Zimmerman's fresco opens a sunroof to the heavens, where Greek gods cavort. In the sunny center, Apollo drives his chariot to bring the dawn, while bearded Zeus (astride an eagle) and peacock-carrying Juno look on. The rainbow symbolizes the peace brought by the enlightened Wittelsbachs. Around the borders of the painting, notice the fun optical illusions: For example, a painted dog holds a stucco bird in its mouth. The painting's natural setting and joie de vivre reflect the pastoral pleasures enjoyed here at the Wittelsbachs' summer home. At one end of the fresco (away from the windows) lounges a lovely maiden with flowers in her hair: it's Flora, the eponymous nymph who inspired this "nymph's castle"—Nymphenburg.

From here, two wings stretch to the left and right. They're mirror images of one another: antechamber, audience chamber, bedchamber, and private living quarters. Guests would arrive here in the Great Hall for an

The airy Great Hall has views of nature out the windows and also in the painted scenes on the ceiling.

awe-inspiring first impression, then make their way through a series of (also-impressive) waiting rooms for their date with the Wittelsbach nobility.

▸ *The tour continues to the left (as you look out the big windows).*

North Wing (Rooms 2-9)

Breeze quickly through this less interesting wing, filled with tapestries and Wittelsbach portraits (including curly-haired Max Emanuel, who built this wing). Pause in the long corridor lined with paintings of various Wittelsbach palaces. The ones of Nymphenburg show the place around 1720, back when there was nothing but countryside between it and downtown (and gondolas plied the canals). Imagine the logistics when the royal family—with their entourage of 200—decided to move out to the summer palace. Find the painting of Fürstenried Palace (in another Munich suburb), and look for the twin onion domes of the Frauenkirche in the distance.

▸ *Return to the Great Hall and enter the other wing.*

South Wing (Rooms 10-20)

Pass through the gold-and-white Room 10 and turn right into the red-walled Audience Chamber. The room calls up the exuberant time of Nymphenburg's founding couple, Ferdinand and Henriette. A portrait on the wall shows them posing together in their rich courtly dress. Another painting depicts them in a Greek myth: Henriette (as the moon-goddess Diana) leads little Max Emanuel by the hand, while Ferdinand (as her mortal lover Endymion) receives the gift of a sword. The ceiling painting (of the earth goddess Cybele) and the inlaid table also date from the time of Nymphenburg's first family.

▸ *After admiring the Queen's Bedroom and Chinese lacquer cabinet, head down the long hall to...*

King Ludwig I's Gallery of Beauties

The room is decorated top to bottom with portraits of 36 beautiful women (all of them painted by Joseph Stieler between 1827 and 1850). Ludwig I was a consummate girl-watcher. (His rakish coronation portrait—by Stieler—hangs in the Neue Pinakothek.)

Ludwig prided himself on his ability to appreciate beauty regardless of social rank. He enjoyed picking out the prettiest women from the general public and, with one of the most effective pickup lines of all time, invite them to the palace for a portrait. Who could refuse? The portraits were on public display in the Residenz, and catapulted their subjects to stardom. The women range from commoners to princesses, but notice that they share one physical trait—Ludwig obviously preferred brunettes. The portraits are done in the modest and slightly sentimental Biedermeier style popular in central Europe, as opposed to the more flamboyant Romanticism style (so beloved of Ludwig's "mad" grandson) also thriving at that time.

Most of these portraits have rich stories behind them (each of the following are at eye level): Find Helene Sedlmayr, a humble cobbler's daughter who caught Ludwig's eye; she poses in a dress way beyond her budget. Though poor, she was considered Munich's comeliest *Fräulein,* and she eventually married the king's valet and had 10 children. To the left of Helene, Lady Jane Ellenborough Digby—an elegant English baroness—went through four marriages and numerous affairs, including one with Ludwig (and, much later, with his son Otto, after Otto had become king of Greece). She was fluent in nine languages, including Arabic, after marrying a Syrian sheik 20 years her junior.

Lola Montez was the king's most notorious mistress. In 1846, the skirt-chasing Ludwig was beguiled by this dancer from Ireland. The portrait shows her the year she met Ludwig (she was 29, he was 60), wearing the black-lace mantilla and red flowers of a Spanish dancer. Lola became

Lady Digby, one of Ludwig I's mistresses   Lola Montez, who proved Ludwig's undoing

his mistress, and he fawned over her in public, scandalizing Munich. The Münchners resented her spending their tax money and dominating their king (supposedly inspiring the phrase "Whatever Lola wants, Lola gets"). In 1848, as Europe was swept by a tide of revolution, the citizens rose up and forced Ludwig to abdicate.

(And where in the "gallery of beauties" is the portrait of Ludwig's wife, Queen Therese? She's not here...you'll have to duck into the elegant, green Queen's Study to see her portrait.) Near Lola, find Princess Marie of Prussia—Ludwig's daughter-in-law—who once lived in the last rooms we'll visit.

▶ *Pass through the blue Audience Room (with elaborate curtain rods and mahogany furniture in the French-inspired Empire style) and into the (other)...*

Queen's Bedroom

The room has much the same furniture it had on August 25, 1845, when Princess Marie gave birth to the future King Ludwig II. Little Ludwig (see his bust, next to brother Otto's) was greatly inspired by Nymphenburg— riding horses in summer, taking sleigh rides in winter, reading poetry at Amalienburg. The love of nature and solitude he absorbed at Nymphenburg eventually led Ludwig to abandon Munich for his castles in the remote Bavarian countryside. By the way, note the mirror in this bedroom. Royal births were carefully witnessed, and the mirror allowed for a better view. While Ludwig's birth was well-documented, his death was shrouded in mystery (see page 122).

▶ *When you're ready to leave the palace, there's much more to see on the grounds and in the outlying buildings. First up: the Royal Stables Museum—to the left of the main palace (as you approach the complex).*

Royal Stables Museum (Marstallmuseum)

These former stables are full of gilded coaches that will make you think of Cinderella's journey to the king's ball. In the big entrance hall is a golden carriage drawn by eight fake white horses. In 1742, it carried Karl Albrecht Wittelsbach to Frankfurt to be crowned Holy Roman Emperor. As emperor, he got eight horses—kings got only six. The event is depicted in a frieze on the museum wall; Karl's carriage is #159.

Other objects bear witness to the good times of the relaxed Nymphenburg lifestyle. You'll see the sleigh of Max Emanuel, decorated with a carved Hercules. A carousel (not always on display) was for the royal kids.

Next up are things owned by Ludwig II—several sleighs, golden carriages, and (in the glass cases) harnesses—as well as portraits of the king. In another hall are more practical coaches for everyday use, and—at the far end—Ludwig II's favorite horse, "Cosa-Rara," stuffed and mounted.

Upstairs is a collection of Nymphenburg porcelain, made for the royal family on the premises in their private factory (which is still in operation today). You'll see plates and cups painted in various styles, from ancient Greek to Old Masters, Romantic, and Art Nouveau.

The Rest of the Palace Grounds

Behind the palace is a park pleasant for strolling or finding a bench for a low-profile picnic. There are several small buildings you can visit—a bathhouse (Badenburg), pagoda (Pagodenburg), and fake ruins (Magdalenenklause).

The most important sight is the hunting lodge called **Amalienburg.** It's 300 yards from the main palace, hiding in the park (head into the sculpted garden and veer to the left, following signs). This little Rococo palace (which takes just a few minutes to tour) was built in 1734 by Elector Karl Albrecht for his wife, Maria Amalia. Like the palace's Great Hall, Amalienburg was designed by François de Cuvilliés and decorated by Johann Baptist Zimmermann. The facade—with a pink-and-white grand entryway—is graced by an image of Diana, goddess of the hunt, flanked by satyrs.

Inside, you get a sense of how the Wittelsbachs loved to hunt. Doghouses under gun cupboards fill the first room. In the fine yellow-and-silver bedroom, the bed is flanked by portraits of Karl Albrecht and Maria Amalia—decked out in hunting attire. She liked her dogs. The door under the portrait leads to stairs to the rooftop. From up there, the queen would shoot pheasants stirred up by the dogs—like skeet shooting.

The mini-Hall of Mirrors is a blue-and-silver commotion of Rococo nymphs designed by Cuvilliés. In the next room, paintings depict court festivities, and formal hunting parties.

As you wander the rest of the **palace grounds,** keep in mind that Nymphenburg Palace was the Wittelsbachs' "getaway" from the stresses of modern life. The grounds were the getaway from their getaway. It's here that they could take off their crowns and royal robes and enjoy being ordinary folks enjoying simple pleasures in the best that nature had to offer.

Dachau Concentration Camp Memorial Tour

KZ-Gedenkstätte Dachau

Dachau was the first Nazi concentration camp (1933). Today, it's easily accessible for travelers and an effective voice from our recent but grisly past, pleading "Never again."

A visit here is a powerful and valuable experience and, when approached thoughtfully, well worth the trouble. Many people come away with more respect for history and the dangers of mixing fear, the promise of jobs, blind patriotism, and an evil government. You'll likely see lots of students here, as all Bavarian schoolchildren are required to visit a concentration camp.

It's interesting to think that little more than a couple of generations ago, people greeted each other with a robust *"Sieg Heil!"* Today, almost no Germans know the lyrics of their national anthem, and German flags are a rarity outside of major soccer matches.

Dachau, located eight miles northwest of the city center, is easily reached on public transportation and makes a worthwhile half-day trip.

ORIENTATION

Cost and Hours: Free, daily 9:00-17:00. Some areas of the camp may begin to close before 17:00—plan to wrap up by 16:40 to allow time to exit.

Planning Your Time: Allow yourself about five hours—giving you at least 2.5 hours at the camp, plus round-trip travel from central Munich. With limited time you could do the whole trip in as little as 3.5 hours by concentrating on the museum.

Getting There: The camp is a 45-minute trip from downtown Munich. Take the S-2 (direction: Petershausen) from any central S-Bahn stop (3/hour, 20-minute trip from Hauptbahnhof). At Dachau station, go down the stairs, and follow the crowds out to the bus platforms; find the platform marked *KZ-Gedenkstätte-Concentration Camp Memorial Sight.* Here, catch bus #726 and ride it seven minutes to the KZ-Gedenkstätte stop (3/hour), where you'll see the visitors center. Before you leave this bus stop, note the return times back to the station. To return to Munich, you'll catch the S-2 again at Dachau station (direction: Erding or Markt Schwaben).

The Munich XXL day pass covers the entire trip, both ways (see page 166). With a three-day Munich transport pass, you must buy and stamp additional single tickets (€2.60/person each way) to cover the part of the trip in the green zone.

Drivers follow Dachauer Strasse from downtown Munich to Dachau-Ost, then follow *KZ-Gedenkstätte* signs.

You could also get there via a guided tour from Munich that covers both public transportation and a guide—try Radius Tours (www.radiustours.com) or Munich Walk (www.munichwalktours.de).

Information: The €3.50 audioguide available from visitors center is good but not essential, as the camp is fully labeled in English. The 2.5-hour

English guided tours (€3) leave from the visitors center daily at 11:00 and 13:00 (can fill up in summer, especially at 13:00). Tel. 08131/669-970, www.kz-gedenkstaette-dachau.de.

THE TOUR BEGINS

As you approach the camp on bus #726, you pass through the **town of Dachau**—quiet, tree-lined, and residential—much more pleasant than its unfortunate association with the camp on its outskirts. With 40,000 residents and quick access to downtown Munich, Dachau is now a high-priced and in-demand place to live.

Get off at the KZ-Gedenkstätte bus stop, where you'll see the **visitors center,** which stands outside the camp wall. It doesn't have any exhibits, but does have a small cafeteria (sandwiches and pasta dishes), a book-store with a modest selection of English-language books on Holocaust themes, and a WC (more WCs inside the camp). At the information desk, you can rent an audioguide or sign up for a tour.

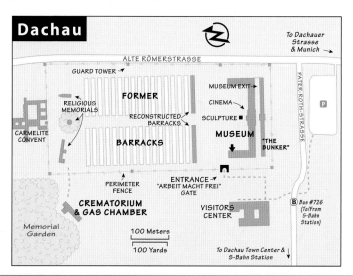

From the visitors center, approach the main compound, surrounded by a thick high wall. You enter, like the inmates did, through the infamous **iron gate** that held the taunting slogan *Arbeit macht frei* ("Work makes you free"). Dachau was a work camp, where prisoners were expected to purge their sins against society through hard labor. This phrase—concocted by the commandant of Dachau—was eventually posted over many Nazi concentration camps, most notoriously at Auschwitz in Poland. Prisoners inevitably learned it was an empty promise. (The original sign was stolen in 2014; a replica may be on display.)

▶ *Step through the gate into the camp grounds. Inside are the four key experiences of the memorial: the museum (just to your right), the bunker (behind the museum), the restored barracks (to your left), and a pensive walk (heading far to your left) across the huge but now-empty camp to the memorials and crematorium at the far end. Enter the museum.*

The Museum

The museum is housed in a former camp maintenance building, one of the few original buildings still standing. The small bookshop helps fund

"Work makes you free"… the empty promise inmates saw as they entered Dachau

the camp, selling a helpful information sheet (€0.50) or excellent 200-page book with CD (€15). Check show times for the museum's powerful 22-minute documentary film.

The museum is organized chronologically, everything is thoughtfully described in English, and computer touchscreens let you watch early newsreels.

Rooms 1-2—The Camp is Founded: On January 30, 1933, Adolf Hitler took power. Two months later, Dachau opened. It was a "concentration" camp, to gather together and isolate enemies of the state, so they could not infect the rest of society. The camp was built well outside Dachau's residential zone, surrounded by a mile-wide restricted area.

A map of the Nazi camp system shows that Dachau was just one of many such camps. Some were concentration camps (marked with a square, like Dachau). Others (marked with a triangle with a "V") were extermination camps—Auschwitz, Sobibor—built with the express purpose of executing people on a mass scale. Nearby, photos and posters chronicle the rise of Hitler in the 1920s: the resentment bred by Germany's defeat in World War I, the weak Weimar Republic, Hitler's solution to Germany's problems (blame the Jews), his failed Beer Hall Putsch, his participation in mainstream politics. No sooner did he take power than he suspended democracy and began squelching all opposition.

Rooms 3-7—Life at the Camp: In 1933, the first prisoners passed through the *Arbeit macht frei* gates. They were classified and labeled with a badge (see the chart on page 76) according to their "crime" against the state. Besides political activists (communists and leftist intellectuals), prisoners included homosexuals, Jehovah's Witnesses, Gypsies, so-called career criminals, and Germans who had tried to flee the country. A special badge—the yellow star of David—was reserved for a group the Nazis particularly loathed, Jews.

The camp was run by the SS, the organization (headed by mastermind Heinrich Himmler) charged with Germany's internal security. Dachau was a training center for future camp managers. Rudolf Höss, who worked at Dachau from 1934 to 1938, went on to become the first commandant of Auschwitz.

Life at Dachau was horrific. It was a work camp, where inmates were expected to pay for their "crimes" with slave labor. It was strictly regimented: a wake-up call at 4:00, an 11-hour workday, roll call at 5:15 and 19:00, lights out at 21:00. The work was hard, whether quarrying or hauling loads

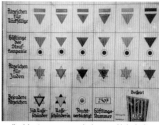

As soon as Hitler took power…   …dissidents were rounded up and labeled.

or constructing the very buildings you see today. The rations were meager. Rule-breakers were punished severely—all manner of torture took place here. The most common punishment was being forced to stand at attention until you collapsed.

On September 1, 1939, Germany invaded Poland, World War II began, and Dachau's role changed.

Cinema: The 22-minute film, dating from the 1960s, is a sobering, graphic, and sometimes grisly account of the rise of Hitler and the atrocities of the camp (English showings generally at 10:00, 11:30, 12:30, 14:00, and 15:00; not recommended for children under 12).

Rooms 8-15—The War Years: Once the war began, conditions at Dachau deteriorated. The original camp had been designed to hold just under 3,000 inmates. In 1937 and 1938, the camp was expanded and the building that now houses the museum was built, as well as barracks intended to hold 6,000 prisoners. With the war, the prisoner population swelled, and the Nazis found other purposes for the camp. It was less a concentration camp for German dissidents and more a dumping ground for foreigners and POWs. It was used as a special prison for 2,000 Catholic priests. From Dachau, Jewish prisoners were sent east to the gas chambers. Inmates were put to use as slave labor for the German war machine—many were shipped to nearby camps to make armaments. Prisoners were used as human guinea pigs for war-related medical experiments of human tolerance for air pressure, hypothermia, and biological agents like malaria; the photos of these victims may be the most painful to view.

As the Allies closed in on both fronts, Dachau was bursting with more than 30,000 prisoners jammed into its 34 barracks. Disease broke out, and food ran short in the winter of 1944-1945. With coal for the crematorium

Prisoners at Dachau were subject to torture, such as standing at attention for long periods.

running low, the corpses of those who died were buried in mass graves outside the camp site. The Allies arrived on April 29. Even so, 2,000 prisoners were so weak or sick that they died soon after. After 12 years in existence, Dachau was finally liberated.

Postscript: About 32,000 people died in Dachau between 1933 and 1945. (By comparison, more than a million were killed at Auschwitz.) But Dachau remains notorious because it was the Nazis' first camp. Oddly, Dachau actually housed people longer *after* the war than during the war. First, it housed Nazi officials arrested by the Allies, as they awaited trial at Nürnberg for war crimes. From 1948 to 1964, the camp became cheap housing for ethnic Germans expelled from Eastern Europe, complete with a cinema, shops, and so on. The last of the barracks was torn down in 1964, and the museum opened the following year.

▶ *Consider using the WC before leaving the museum building (there aren't any bathrooms elsewhere within the camp walls). Find the side door, at the end of the exhibition, which leads out to the long, low bunker behind the museum building.*

Bunker

This was a cellblock for prominent "special prisoners," such as failed Hitler assassins, German religious leaders, and politicians who challenged Nazism. Most of the 136 cells are empty, but exhibits in a few of them (near the entrance) profile the inmates and the SS guards who worked at Dachau, and allow you to listen to some inmates' testimonies. Cell #2 was the interrogation room. Cell #9 was a "standing cell"—inmates were tortured here by being forced to stay on their feet for days at a time.

▶ *Exit the bunker, and walk around past the* Arbeit macht frei *gate to*

Many prisoners were worked to death.

Others were tortured in the bunker cells.

Memorials dot the empty grounds, where visitors can ponder the camp and its motto: "Never Again."

the big square between the museum and the reconstructed barracks, which was used for roll call. In front of the museum, notice the powerful **memorial** *to the victims created in 1968 by Nandor Glid, a Jewish Ho-locaust survivor and artist, which includes humanity's vow: Never Again. Cross the square to the farther of the two reconstructed...*

Barracks

Take a quick look inside to get an idea of what sleeping and living conditions were like in the camp. There were 34 barracks, each measuring about 10 yards by 100 yards. When the camp was at its fullest, there was only about one square yard of living space per inmate.

▶ *Now walk between the two reconstructed barracks and down the tree-lined path past the foundations of the other barracks. It's a long, thoughtful walk, but you soon reach the...*

Sights at the Far End of the Camp

At the end of the camp, in space that once housed the camp vegetable garden, rabbit farm, and brothel, there are now three **religious memorials**—places of meditation and worship (Jewish to your right, Catholic straight ahead, and Protestant to your left). Beyond them, just outside the camp, is a Carmelite convent.

▶ *Turn left toward the corner of the camp and find the small bridge leading to the...*

Camp Crematorium: A memorial garden surrounds the two camp crematorium buildings, which were used to burn the bodies of prisoners who had died or been killed.

The newer, larger concrete crematorium was built to replace the smaller wooden one. One of its rooms is a **gas chamber,** which worked on the same principles as the much larger one at Auschwitz, and was originally disguised as a shower room (the fittings are gone now). It was never put to use at Dachau for mass murder, but some historians suspect that a few people were killed in it experimentally.

The Russian Orthodox shrine in the garden honors the many Russian POWs who died at Dachau.

▶ *To return to Munich, retrace your steps. Exit through the* Arbeit macht frei *gate and turn left, returning to the bus stop where bus #726 takes you back to the Dachau train station. From there, catch the S-2 (direction: Erding or Markt Schwaben) to downtown Munich.*

More Munich Sights

The best sightseeing on a trip to Munich is to take my Munich City Walk and visit the sights detailed in this book's various tour chapters: the ✪ **Residenz,** the ✪ **Museum Quarter,** ✪ **Nymphenburg Palace,** and ✪ **Dachau.**

But don't stop there. In this chapter, I've highlighted the best of Munich's secondary sights. You can choose from rocket science to topless sunbathers, from hot cars to city history, from a breezy bike ride along the river to the sobering new Nazi Documentation Center. Thanks to the city's excellent public transportation system, even outlying sights are less than a half-hour away. None of the sights in this chapter are crowded enough to require making a reservation.

Near Marienplatz

▲Munich City Museum (Münchner Stadtmuseum)

The museum's permanent exhibit on Munich's history is called "Typically Munich!" Use the following mini-tour for an overview, then supplement it with the included audioguide and English booklet. Skip the more expensive temporary-exhibit ticket.

Start in the **ticketing hall** with the wooden model showing Munich today. Find the Frauenkirche, Isar River, New Town Hall, Residenz...and no skyscrapers. The city looks remarkably similar in scale to the model (in the next room) from 1570.

Ground Floor—Medieval: A big gray statue of Henry the Lion introduces us to the city's 12th-century founder. The eight statues of Morris dancers (1480) became a symbol of the vibrant market town (and the tradition continued with the New Town Hall glockenspiel's dancing coopers). On the rest of the ground floor, paintings, armor, and swords capture more medieval ambience.

Munich City Museum's 1,000 years of history includes traditions that survive today, like dancing coopers.

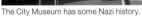
The City Museum has some Nazi history. The Nazi Documentation Center has more.

First Floor—1800s: The "New Munich" was created when the city was expanded beyond the old medieval walls (see the illuminated view of the city from 1761 in the "Canaletto-Blick"). The city was prosperous, as evidenced by the furniture and paintings on display. In the center of the room, find big paintings ("Effigies") of the century's magnificent kings—Maximilian I, Ludwig I, and Ludwig II (as well as Lola Montez, Ludwig I's most famous mistress).

Second Floor—Munich 1900: As Munich approached its 700th birthday, it was a city of artists (Wagner operas, Lenbach portraits), *Jugendstil* furniture, beer, and a cosmopolitan outlook (see the big barrel-shaped peep show of African/Asian peoples). But after the destruction of World War I, Munich became (as seen in the "revue" room) a hotbed of discontent: communists, capitalists, Nazis, and the anarchic theater of comedian Karl Valentin and playwright Bertolt Brecht.

Third Floor—Puppet Theater: You'll see marionettes, Punch-and-Judy hand puppets, and paper cutouts of this unique Bavarian art form.

Back on the second floor, finish with a kaleidoscope of images capturing the contemporary Munich scene—rock music, World Cup triumphs, beer gardens, and other things that are..."typically Munich."

National Socialism Wing: Your permanent-collection ticket includes this small but worthwhile exhibit of photos and uniforms that takes you chronologically through the Nazi years, focused on Munich: the post-WWI struggles, Hitler's 1923 Beer Hall Putsch, his writing of *Mein Kampf,* the mass rallies in Königsplatz and Odeonsplatz, establishment of the Dachau concentration camp, and the destruction rained on Munich in World War II.

▶ *€4, Tue-Sun 10:00-18:00, closed Mon, St.-Jakobs-Platz 1, tel. 089/2332-2370, www.stadtmuseum-online.de. The Servus Heimat souvenir shop*

Nazism in Munich

From its very beginnings, the National Socialist Party was linked with Bavaria. It was in Munich that Hitler and other disillusioned WWI veterans gathered to lick their wounds. The Nazi Party was founded here in 1919, and this is where Hitler staged his attempted coup (the 1923 Beer Hall Putsch). In nearby Landsberg, he was imprisoned and wrote his *Mein Kampf* manifesto.

As soon as the Nazis took power (in 1933), they opened their first concentration camp, outside Munich in Dachau. Munich was the site of the infamous failed peace pact, the Munich Agreement of 1938, where Britain's prime minister tried to avoid war by appeasing Hitler. Once in power, Hitler officially proclaimed Munich "Capital of the Movement."

is fun, and the museum's Stadt Café is good. For location, see the map on page 16.

In the Museum Quarter

▲▲Nazi Documentation Center

Munich was the birthplace of Nazism, and—even after the Nazis took power and moved to Berlin—it remained the official Nazi Party headquarters.

This new center documents the rise and fall of Nazism, with a focus on Munich's role and the reasons behind it. Munich, like the rest of Germany, is determined to learn from its 20th-century nightmare. The center is housed in a stark, light-filled, cube-shaped building located in the heart of what was once a neighborhood of Nazi offices.

A stone's throw from the Documentation Center are other Nazi locales. Königsplatz—a vast expanse enclosed by grandiose Neoclassical buildings—served as the perfect stage for Nazi spectacles. Mass rallies were held here, where they burned forbidden books. (Remember, too, that

Hitler fancied himself an artist, so this area of museums and art academies perfectly suited Hitler's ego.) At the height of Hitler's power, some 50 buildings in the neighborhood housed dozens of Nazi departments and thousands of employees. Most of the Nazi-built architecture is gone now, but at Arcisstrasse 12, once the Führerbau (*"Führer* building," now used as a music academy), you can still see the window of Hitler's personal office above the entrance porch. And the official Nazi Party headquarters (called the Brown House) was next door, along Brienner Strasse. That structure was destroyed in World War II and has now been replaced by a brand-new building—the Nazi Documentation Center.

▶ *€5 includes well-done and techie audioguide; Tue-Sun 10:00-19:00, closed Mon; Brienner Strasse 34, U-2; Königsplatz, tel 089/2336-7001, www.ns-dokumentationszentrum-muenchen.de. For location, see the map on page 7.*

Near the River

▲English Garden (Englischer Garten)

Munich's "Central Park" is the largest urban park on the Continent (established 1789). It stretches north for three miles—a vast expanse of lawns, groves, lakes, and streams laced with bike paths and dotted with a few museums. More than 100,000 locals commune with nature here on sunny summer days. It's great for a walk, or—better yet—a bike ride (unfortunately, there are no bike rentals in the park; see page 168 for a list of bike-rental places).

For the best quick visit, start at the south end, where the English Garden touches the Old Town. (Take bus #100 or tram #18 to the Nationalmuseum/Haus der Kunst stop.) At the garden entrance stands the **Haus der Kunst** (www.hausderkunst.de). This "house of art"—a bold and fascist building—was built by Hitler as a temple of Nazi art. Now it houses temporary exhibits (ironically, the kind of art that annoyed the Führer most—modern). Alongside the Haus der Kunst (where Prinzregentenstrasse crosses a canal), you can watch **surfers** riding the rapids of a river.

Follow the path downstream into the English Garden. Walk up the small hill topped with a little temple **(Monopteros)** for a postcard view of the city. Continue on to the big **Chinese Tower** beer garden for refreshment. Afterward, you could retrace your steps, or walk northwest 600

More Munich Sights

1 Kilometer

1 Mile

To Dachau

BMW-WELT & MUSEUM

FRANKFURTER-RING

A-9

TOWER

PETUEL - RING

Olympic Park

To Rothenburg & Romantic Road

A-8

VERDISTR.

DACHAUER STRASSE

WINTRICH-RING

99

NYMPHENBURG PALACE & GARDENS

304

ARNULF STR.

MAIN TRAIN STATION

CHINESE TOWER BEER GARDEN

English Garden

LEOPOLDSTR.

UNGERERSTR.

See detail maps

OLD CITY

PRINZREGENTENSTR.

VILLA VON STUCK

A-94

LANDSBERGERSTR.

To Landsberg & Füssen (via Romantic Road)

MUSEUM OF TRANSPORTATION

OKTOBERFEST SITE (THERESIENWIESE)

99

BOSCH.

LINDWURM STR.

Isar River

DEUTSCHES MUSEUM

ROSEN-HEIMER

CHIEMGAUSTR.

A-96 To Landsberg, Füssen (via Romantic Road) & Lindau

A-95 To Andechs Monastery & Garmisch

A-8

A-995

99

To Salzburg

yards (or take bus #54 a couple stops) to the Giselastrasse U-Bahn station and return to town on the U-3 or U-6.

Caution: The park is sprinkled with buck-naked sunbathers—quite a shock to prudish Americans (they're the ones riding their bikes into the river and trees).

Nearby: The tired **Bavarian National Museum** (www.bayerisches-nationalmuseum.de) and **Villa Stuck,** former home of Munich's top Art Nouveau artist (www.villastuck.de), are nearby.

▲Deutsches Museum

Enjoy wandering through vast rooms of historic airplanes, spaceships,

The Chinese Tower in the English Garden

An early computer in the Deutsches Museum

mining, the harnessing of wind and water power, hydraulics, musical instruments, printing, chemistry, computers, astronomy, and nanotechnol-
ogy...it's the Louvre of technical know-how. The museum feels a bit dated,
but major renovations are under way (though a number of exhibits may be
closed during your visit—check ahead).

Get your bearings in **Room 10,** just past the ticket-taker. This high-
ceilinged room is dominated by the tall-masted ship, *Maria*. Downstairs
is the first German *U-Boot* (undersea boat). Above you in Room 10 hang
early airships (best seen from the first floor), including zeppelins, a Wright
Brothers plane from 1909, and a Fokker tri-plane made famous by the Red
Baron. Behind you, locate the handy elevator—it's one of the few elevators
in this labyrinthine building that goes to all six floors. Now, explore.

From Room 10, continue straight ahead to spacious **Room 18,** filled
with airplanes, helicopters, jets, and the European-built Spacelab capsule
that went up on the US Space Shuttle *Columbia* in 1993. In the far right
corner (Rooms 11-16 and 25) is new technology—DNA, nano-technology,
and robotics. **Room 9** has twice-daily high-voltage demonstrations showing the noisy creation of a five-foot bolt of lightning.

The **upper floors** are equally interesting—here's a sample: prehis-
toric cave paintings and glass-blowing (second floor, Rooms 39-40), and
a 1956 Univac computer (third floor, Rooms 52-53) as big as a room, with
a million components, costing a million dollars, and with less computing
power than your smartphone. The astronomy exhibits and planetarium
(floors 4-6, reached by that elevator by Room 10) are excellent. You finally
emerge on the museum's **rooftop,** the "sundial garden" (Room 64); on a
clear day, you can see the Alps.

▶ €11, €16 combo-ticket includes Museum of Transportation (see next

The Museum of Transportation

BMW-Welt is a fancy car showroom.

page) as well as a Flight Museum, daily 9:00-17:00, several small cafés in the museum, tel. 089/21791, www.deutsches-museum.de.

Getting There: Take tram #16 to the Deutsches Museum stop, or the S-Bahn to Isartor. Then walk 300 yards over the river, following signs. (The entrance is near the far end of the building.)

Outside the Center

▲Museum of Transportation (Verkehrszentrum)

With just enough to interest the casual visitor, this place is heaven for any driving enthusiast. It's housed in three giant hangar-like exhibition halls. Hall I, about urban transport, features a 1927 S-Bahn subway car. Hall II is trains and buses, like the Maffei steam engine that could go 80 miles per hour, and the 1950s panorama bus that shuttled eager tourists to Italy. Hall III is all about fun: motorcycles, bicycles, skis, and race cars, like early Mercedes-Benz and "Grand Prix" race cars.

▶ *€6, daily 9:00-17:00, take U-4 or U-5 to the Schwanthalerhöhe stop, museum is a few steps away at Theresienhöhe 14a, tel. 089/500-806-123, www.deutsches-museum.de.*

▲▲BMW-Welt and Museum

This is the world headquarters of the Bavarian Motor Works, or BMW ("beh-em-VEH" to Germans). Beamer dreamers can explore this space-age complex of buildings to learn more about this brand's storied heritage.

The futuristic, bowl-shaped **BMW Museum** encloses a world of floating walkways and exhibits highlighting BMW products through the years. First came airplane engines (1917), then motorcycles, then the first

BMW sedan in 1929. Sleek design was celebrated from the start, whether in motorsports, roadsters, or luxury cars. The 1956 BMW 507 is enough to rev anyone's engine.

BMW-Welt ("BMW World")—a cloud-shaped, glass-and-steel architectural masterpiece—is the showroom. It's free and filled with interactive exhibits and high-powered videos designed to fuel potential customers' dreams. Besides today's models, you get a breathtaking look into the future.

The actual **headquarters** (in the building nicknamed "the Four Cylinders") is not open to the public, and the **factory** is only tourable with a months-in-advance reservations (see the website).

▶ *Museum—€9, Tue-Sun 10:00-18:00, closed Mon, tel. 089/125-016-001, www.bmw-welt.com. BMW-Welt—free, building open daily 7:30-24:00, exhibits 9:00-18:00. English tours are offered of both the museum (€12, 1.5 hours, call ahead for times) and BMW-Welt (€7, daily at 14:00, 80 minutes). Factory tours are €8 (2.5 hours, Mon-Fri only, book at least 2*

The BMW Museum (with the Olympic Park tower behind) displays stylish cars in modern buildings.

months in advance at 089/125-016-001, or ask about last-minute cancellations, info at www.bmw-werk-muenchen.de).

__Getting There:__ It's very easy: Ride the U-3 to Olympia-Zentrum; the stop faces the BMW-Welt entry (with the museum just beyond). On a bike, it's easily reached, and well-signed, from the English Garden.

Olympic Park (Olympiapark München)

Munich hosted the 1972 Olympics. Today the grounds are worthwhile for the pleasant park, striking "cobweb" style stadium, 820-foot view tower (Olympiaturm), and excellent swimming pool.

▸ *Tower—€5.50, daily 9:00-24:00, tel. 089/30670, www.olympiapark.de. Pool—€4.40, daily 7:00-23:00, tel. 089/2361-5050, www.swm.de. The U-3 runs from Marienplatz directly to the Olympia-Zentrum stop.*

▲Bike Rides

Green, bike-friendly Munich has some nice joyrides you could take on a rental bike, including into the surrounding countryside. For details, see page 168.

Day Trips from Munich

The best day trips are Neuschwanstein Castle (see page 113) and Salzburg (see page 133), but there are other sights within striking distance.

Nürnberg, easily reached by fast train (2-3/hour, 1-1.5 hours), is known for its glorious medieval architecture, haunting Nazi past, interesting Germanic history museum, and Germany's tiniest bratwurst (www.tourismus.nuernberg.de).

The **Andechs Monastery** offers a fine Baroque church in a rural Bavarian setting at a monastery that serves hearty cafeteria-quality food—and perhaps the best beer in Germany. To get there (1.5 hours), take the S-8 to Herrsching, and catch bus #951 (free to enter, *Biergarten* open daily 10:00-20:00, tel. 08152/3760, www.andechs.de).

If you have more time, the **Romantic Road bus** (mid-April-late Oct only) is a slow, scenic joyride that connects Munich's central bus station (ZOB) to several cute towns as it makes its way through Füssen, Augsburg, Dinkelsbühl, Rothenburg, Würzburg, Frankfurt, and other destinations en route (schedule at www.romantic-road.com).

Sleeping

Unless you hit Munich during a business convention or big holiday, you can find a fine double with breakfast in a good basic hotel for €100. I've grouped my hotel listings into three neighborhoods: near the **train station** (less atmospheric, but better values and near transportation options); in the **Old Town,** south of Marienplatz (pricier, but closer to sights, shopping, nightlife, and Munich's pedestrian-friendly ambience); and **outside the Old Town** (good-value finds a short walk or tram ride away from the action).

I like hotels that are clean, central, good-value, friendly, run with a respect for Bavarian traditions, and small enough to have a hands-on owner and stable staff. Four of these six virtues means it's a keeper. Double rooms listed in this book average around €110 (including a private bathroom). They range from a low of roughly €65 (very simple, with toilet and shower down the hall) to €220 (maximum plumbing and more).

A Typical Munich Hotel Room

A typical €110 double room in Munich will be small by American standards. It will have one double bed (either queen-sized or slightly narrower) or two twins. There's probably a bathroom in the room with a toilet, sink, and bathtub or shower. The room has a telephone and TV, and may have a safe. Single rooms, triples, and quads will have similar features.

Many of my listings are in old buildings—charming, yes, but also somewhat creaky, with steep stairs (and possibly no elevator). Don't judge the hotel by its entryway alone: Many smaller pensions are on the building's upper floor, with cheery rooms. Air-conditioning is not the norm at this price, but fans are usually available. In summer, when you may need to open windows, consider street noise and ask about quieter rooms in back. Some hotels still allow smoking, so ask about non-smoking rooms when you book. The staff speaks English.

Breakfast—often included in the room price—might be as little as bread and coffee, but is usually a self-serve buffet with cereal, ham, cheese, yogurt, and juice. The hotel will have Internet access, either Wi-Fi or a public terminal in the lobby. At most of my listings, at least one of these options is free. If Wi-Fi is crucial to you, get specific, e.g., "In the room?"

German hotels have some regional quirks. A "double bed" and "two twin beds" are sometimes the same thing—two twin mattresses pushed together. Instead of blankets, your bed may have a comforter. To open and close windows, experiment with the handle to discover the three positions: fully closed, fully open, or propped open from the top. In the elevator, press "E" for the ground floor. A few traditional hotels offer the option of half-board *(Halbpension),* which includes dinner. Energy-conscious German hoteliers appreciate you turning off unused lights and avoiding endless showers.

Making Reservations

Reserve as far in advance as you can, particularly if you'll be traveling in peak season: April through June and September through October. Munich hotel prices are pretty uniform Monday through Saturday, but Sundays can be cheaper—ask for a discount. Prices can rise 20 percent or more during three-day weekends surrounding holidays (find a list at www.bavaria.us— click on "Events," then "Bavarian Legal Holidays") and during business

Hotel Price Code

$$$	Most rooms are €130 or more.
$$	Most rooms between €90-130.
$	Most rooms €90 or less.

These rates are for a standard double room with bath (outside of conventions or holidays); most include breakfast. Verify current rates online or by email. For the best prices, book directly with the hotel.

conventions (check the schedule at www.muenchen.de—search for "Congresses"). Oktoberfest (held late Sept-early Oct, www.oktoberfest. de) is the busiest, when hotels can be booked solid and prices can triple.

Make reservations by phone, through the hotel's website, or with an email that reads something like this:

Dear Hotel Schnitzel,

I would like to reserve a double room for 2 people for 3 nights, arriving 19 July and departing 22 July. If possible, I would like a quiet room (non-smoking) with a double bed (not twin beds), and a shower (not a tub). Please let me know if you have a room available and the price. Thank you.

If they require your credit-card number for a deposit, you can send it by email (I do), but it's safer via phone, the hotel's secure website, or split between two emails. Once your room is booked, print out the confirmation, and reconfirm your reservation with a phone call or email a day or two in advance (alert them if you'll be arriving after 17:00). If canceling a reservation, some hotels require advance notice—otherwise they may bill you. Even if there's no penalty, it's polite to give at least three days' notice.

Budget Tips

To get the best rates, book directly with the hotel, not through a hotel-booking engine. Start with the hotel's website, looking for promo deals. Check rates every few days, because—thanks to automated "dynamic pricing" schemes—a hotel's rates can change greatly, even day-to-day, based on demand. Email several hotels to ask for their best price and compare offers—you may be astonished at the range. Some may give a discount if you stay at least three nights or pay in cash.

Besides hotels, there are cheaper alternatives. A bed-and-breakfast (B&B, called a *Pension, Gasthof,* or *Gasthaus*) offers a personal touch at a fair price—I've listed several. Spare rooms in private homes are advertised as *Zimmer Frei.* I also list a few all-ages hostels, which offer €25 dorm beds (and a few inexpensive doubles) and might come with curfews and other rules. Websites such as www.airbnb.com make it reasonably easy to find a place to sleep in someone's home.

Renting an apartment can save money if you're traveling as a family, staying more than a week, and planning to cook your own meals. Try www.homeaway.com (offering a wide range of listings) or www.vrbo.com (putting you directly in touch with owners).

Don't be too cheap when picking a place to stay. Anything under €80 (even my listings) can be a little rough around the edges. Your Munich experience will be more memorable with a welcoming oasis to call home.

NEAR THE TRAIN STATION: Good-value hotels in un-atmospheric but safe neighborhood with great location for transportation options, south of the station. To some the neighborhood is colorful (multicultural), to others it feels seedy (sex cinemas).

$$$ Marc München Senefelderstrasse 12 tel. 089/559-820 | www.hotel-marc.de	Polished, modern, four-star comfort a half-block from station, best value are "superior king" rooms, air-con
$$ Hotel Monaco Schillerstrasse 9 | tel. 089/545-9940 www.hotel-monaco.de	Homey, friendly, flowery, fresh oasis tucked inside nondescript building, two blocks from station
$$ Hotel Uhland Uhlandstrasse 1 | tel. 089/543-350 www.hotel-uhland.de	Stately family-run mansion in genteel residential neighborhood a bus ride (#58) from station
$$ Hotel Belle Blue Schillerstrasse 21 | tel. 089/550-6260 www.hotel-belleblue.de	Three blocks from the station; 30 comfortable, modern (and blue) rooms, air-con
$$ Hotel Bristol Pettenkoferstrasse 2 | tel. 089/5434-8880 | www.bristol-munich.de	Bright, efficient, business-like, near Sendlinger Tor U-Bahn station
$$ Hotel Deutsches Theater Landwehrstrasse 18 | tel. 089/545-8525 www.hoteldeutschestheater.de	Three-star, brass-and-marble rooms, some night noise from theater
$$ Hotel Europäischer Hof Bayerstrasse 31 | tel. 089/551-510 www.heh.de	Across street from station; huge, impersonal, and decent; best-value rooms are along noisy street
$ Hotel Royal Schillerstrasse 11a | tel. 089/5998-8160 www.hotel-royal.de	Great value though strip joints flank the entry, institutional but fresh and bright, friendly staff
$ Litty's Hotel Landwehrstrasse 32c tel. 089/5434-4211 | www.littyshotel.de	Basic and serviceable, small rooms, personable staff
$ CVJM (YMCA) Landwehrstrasse 13 | tel. 089/552-1410 www.cvjm-muenchen.org/hotel	All ages, basic rooms (singles, doubles, triples, or 3-bed dorms) with shared bathroom
$ Hostels on Senefelderstrasse www.wombats-hostels.eu www.euro-youth-hotel.de www.jaegershostel.de	Three similar hostels with €25 dorm beds for young beer-drinking backpackers, lively nightlife, no curfew, Jaeger's is quietest

Sleeping

IN THE OLD TOWN: This area south of Marienplatz (going toward Sendlinger Tor) is more genteel, closer to sights (e.g., Viktualienmarkt), and pricier.

$$$ Hotel Blauer Bock Sebastiansplatz 9 | tel. 089/231-780 www.hotelblauerbock.de	Historic building with 70 remodeled, classy-if-spartan rooms, great location near City Museum
$$$ Mercure München Altstadt Hotel Hotterstrasse 4 | tel. 089/232-590 www.mercure-muenchen-altstadt.de	Bland chain hotel with reliable modern business-class comforts (air-con), quiet street near Marienplatz
$$$ Derag Livinghotel am Viktualienmarkt Frauenstrasse 4 | tel. 089/885-6560 www.deraghotels.de	Sleek kitchenette suites by Viktualienmarkt, can sometimes nab a double for €170, air-con
$$$ Hotel am Markt Heiliggeiststrasse 6 | tel. 089/225-014 www.hotel-am-markt.eu	Decent if old-feeling, by Viktualienmarkt, can opt out of expensive breakfast
$$$ Hotel Olympic Hans-Sachs-Strasse 4 | tel. 089/231-890 www.hotel-olympic.de	37 fresh, artsy, relaxing rooms near Viktualienmarkt
$$ Hotel am Viktualienmarkt Utzschneiderstrasse 14 tel. 089/231-1090 www.hotel-am-viktualienmarkt.de	Small but well-designed hotel with small rooms on small street, great-value single rooms
$$ Pension Lindner Dultstrasse 1 | tel. 089/263-413 www.pension-lindner.com	Clean and quiet, nine pleasant pastel-bouquet rooms, welcoming owner, book ahead, cash discount
$$ Pension am Jakobsplatz Dultstrasse 1 | tel. 089/2323-1556 www.pension-jakobsplatz.de	Four basic but pleasant rooms, two have shower in room but toilet down the hall
$$ Motel One Sendlinger Tor Herzog-Wilhelm-Strasse 28 tel. 089/5177-7250 www.motel-one.com	Huge chain hotel near convenient Sendlinger Tor U-Bahn, modern-but-small rooms, book ahead, nice streetside views, air-con

A BIT OUTSIDE THE OLD TOWN WALLS: These are an easy tram or subway ride (or 10-minute walk) east or south of the Old Town walls.

$$$ Hotel Admiral Kohlstrasse 9 | tel. 089/216-350 www.hotel-admiral.de	Classy yet homey, near Deutsches Museum
$$ Hotel Isartor Baaderstrasse 2-4 | tel. 089/216-3340 www.hotel-isartor.de	68 comfortable but plain rooms, east of Marienplatz
$$ Hotel Mueller Fliegenstrasse 4 | tel. 89/232-3860 www.hotel-mueller-muenchen.de	Just south of Sendlinger Tor, alpine-bright and sunny, 44 cozy rooms
$$ Carat Hotel Lindwurmstrasse 13 | tel. 089/230-380 www.carat-hotel-muenchen.de	South of Sendlinger Tor, glossy slumber-mill for tour groups, street-side rooms have air-con, apartments have kitchenettes

Sleeping

Eating

Munich is often voted one of Germany's "Most Livable" cities, and one of the reasons is the city's appreciation for good food and drink in casual settings.

Munich's best-known food option is the traditional beer hall. These can range from rowdy oompah wurst-factories to under-the-stars beer gardens to elegant restaurants, so I've offered plenty of suggestions. But Munich also has other dining opportunities. You'll find both budget take-out places and top-notch international cuisine.

My listings are either in the **Old Town** (within a 10-minute walk of Marienplatz) or in the convenient **train station** neighborhood.

No matter where you dine, expect it to be *gemütlich*—a much-prized Bavarian virtue, meaning an atmosphere of relaxed coziness.

Restaurant Price Code

$$$	Most main courses €16 or more
$$	Most main courses €12-16.
$	Most main courses €12 or less.

Based on the average price of a main dish on the menu. Salads, appetizers, and wursts are several euros cheaper, and some places offer lunch specials. A typical meal at a $$ restaurant—including appetizer, main dish, house wine, water, and service—would cost about €30.

When in Germany...

When in Germany, I eat on the German schedule. For breakfast, I eat at the hotel (fresh-baked bread, meat, cheese, Müsli cereal) or grab a pastry and coffee at a bakery. Traditionally, the German lunch (12:00–14:00) has been a big meal (and many restaurants offer lunch specials), though busy Germans today might just grab a sandwich at a bakery. In between meals, you could stop at a take-out stand for a wurst. Bavarians even have a special word for the traditional in-between-meal snack—*Brotzeit* ("Bread time")—a platter of bread with toppings. In the late afternoon, Germans enjoy a beverage with friends at an outdoor table on a lively square. Dinner (18:00-21:00) is the time for slowing down and savoring a quiet multi-course restaurant meal, or combining dinner with beer and fun in a beer hall.

Restaurant Etiquette

Full-service, sit-down restaurants in Germany operate much like restaurants everywhere, but there are a few small differences in etiquette.

Tipping is not necessary (because a 12-15 percent service charge is usually included in the menu price), but a tip of about 10 percent is a nice reward for good service. Germans prefer not leaving coins on the table. So, for a €10 meal, they might tip €1 by paying with a €20 bill and telling the waiter the total they wish to pay: *"Elf Euro"*—"Eleven euros"—to get €9 change.

Germans are willing to pay for bottled water with their meal (*Mineralwasser mit/ohne Gas*—with/without carbonation). You can request tap water *(Leitungswasser),* though your waiter may grumble. A *Stammtisch* sign on a table means it's reserved for regulars. Many eateries offer pleasant outdoor seating in good weather. There's usually no extra charge to sit outside. Bavarian eateries are officially smoke-free indoors.

Most restaurants offer a "menu" or *Tageskarte*—a fixed-price meal—at lunchtime on weekdays. It's typically under €10 for a main course plus side dish. The best dish on any menu is often the house specialty. For smaller portions, order from the *kleine Hunger* (small hunger) section of the menu.

Good service is relaxed service—only a rude waiter will rush you. When you want the bill, say, "*Rechnung* (REKH-nung), *bitte*." To wish others "Happy eating!" offer a cheery "*Guten Appetit!*"

Bakeries, Cafés, and More

Besides fancy restaurants, there are other less-formal places to fill the tank.

Other Restaurants: Places that serve meals go by many names. *Gasthaus, Gasthof, Gaststätte,* and *Gaststube* all loosely describe an informal, inn-type restaurant. A *Keller* (or *Ratskeller*) is an eatery located in a cellar. A beer hall *(Brauhaus),* beer garden *(Biergarten),* or wine cellar *(Weinstube)* will serve basic, traditional meals. Department-store cafeterias (usually on the top floor with a view) are handy.

Cheap Take-out Meals and Picnics: Many Bavarians go to a bakery *(Bäckerei)* for a good, cheap sandwich—either pre-made or order-your-own. Bakeries don't offer full sit-down meals, but they usually have a few tables.

Munich makes it easy to turn a picnic into a first-class affair. Grab something to go and enjoy a bench in a lively square or leafy park. Some beer gardens allow patrons who order a drink to picnic at their tables (on tables without a tablecloth). It's easy to find pre-made sandwiches, take-out salads, and cold cuts at bakeries, butcher shops *(Metzgerei),* and supermarkets. A *Schnell Imbiss* is a small fast-food takeaway stand where you can get a bratwurst and more.

Best of the Wurst: In Germany, you're never far from a Würstelstand (sausage stand). The wurst, usually pork sausage, comes in many varieties. Bratwurst is a generic term that simply means "grilled sausage." A Burenwurst is what we'd call "kielbasa." There's also Bockwurst, Liverwurst, and so on. Generally, the darker the weenie, the spicier it is. Munich's best-known specialty is Weisswurst: Boiled white sausage (peel off the casing before you eat it), served with sweet mustard and a pretzel.

Your wurst comes on a paper plate with your choice of bread *(Brot)* or roll *(Semmel)*, and with ketchup or mustard—sweet *(süss)* or sharp *(scharf)*. Locals don't always put the sausage in the bread like a hot dog. For some varieties they take a bite of sausage, then a bite of bread. ("That's why you have two hands.")

Snack Foods: Pretzels *(Brezel* or—in Bavaria—*Brez'n)*, either plain or buttered, make for an inexpensive snack. A menu item called *Brotzeit* ("bread time") is a wooden platter of bread with various toppings: cold cuts, meat spreads (like *Leberwurst,* made from liver), *Obatzda* (pungent cheese spread), *Kartoffelkäse* (spread made of mashed potatoes), pickles, and radishes.

Ethnic: All schnitzeled out? An Asian rice or noodle dish, a freshly baked pizza, or a Turkish sandwich will cost you only €4-7. Originally from Turkey, *Döner Kebab* (sliced meat and vegetables served in pita bread) has become a classic take-out meal for Germans. Beyond the basic *Döner,* there's *Döner Teller* (on a plate with side dishes), falafel (chickpea croquettes), "Turkish pizzas," and more.

Beer Halls and Beer Gardens

One of Munich's great experiences is drinking some of the world's best beer in a vast indoor beer hall *(Brauhaus)* or outdoor beer garden *(Biergarten)*—many establishments offer both seating options. Here, the beer comes in big steins, meals are inexpensive, white radishes are salted and cut in delicate spirals, and surly beer maids quickly clear the tables. Closed days disappear during Oktoberfest, when most places are open daily.

Beer gardens began back when monks brewed beer, stored in cellars

Turkish Döner Kebabs are everywhere.

A *Mass* of *Helles* is the classic beer order.

beneath courtyards kept cool by the shade of chestnut trees. Eventually, tables were set up for the buying public, and these convivial eateries evolved. Beer halls have a long tradition as the social hub of the community. In the days before radio, politicians came here to connect with the public. Munich's Hofbräuhaus was the first place where Hitler addressed a big crowd.

Ordering Etiquette: Most beer halls are informal places where you can seat yourself, often at big shared tables. Don't sit at tables marked *Stammtisch*—they're reserved.

In some places, a waiter comes around, and you order your food and drink from a menu, like in a restaurant. But in vast beer gardens, it's usually self-serve. (*Selbstbedienung* means self-service, and *Bedienung* means table service, and many beer halls will have separate sections.) At a self-service beer garden, you grab an empty glass from the rack, pay a €1 deposit *(Pfand),* and get a token for a refund when you return the glass. Then, go to a beer-filling station to choose your beer, pay the man, and get your glass filled up.

For food, large beer gardens have a self-service cafeteria system, where you assemble your dream feast by visiting various counters—get your roast chicken here, your pork shoulder there, your salad bar there. The displays make it easy to just point to what you want. You pay at each counter (they're separate vendors). After the meal, bus your dirty dishes at the station marked *Geschirrabgabe.*

Beer: The average German drinks 40 gallons of beer a year and has a tremendous variety to choose from. *Flaschenbier* is bottled, and *vom Fass* is on tap. Huge liter mugs of tap beer (called *ein Mass* in German) cost about €8. A half-liter is *eine Halbe.* In some places, if you order *eine Halbe,* the barmaid might say, "Why don't you come back when you're thirsty?"

Most Bavarian beers fall into four categories: *Helles* is an American-style lager, served in a mug. *Dunkles* (Munich-style) is dark, sweet, and malty. *Weissbier* (what Americans call "Hefeweizen") is a yeasty, wheat-based beer, with a frothy head, served in a tall glass with a wedge of lemon. Other Bavarian specialties are *Bockbier* (a high-alcohol, hoppy, bittersweet amber) and *Märzenbier* (a light, malty, and highly alcoholic lager brewed in March to be ready for Oktoberfest). A *Radler* is a refreshing half-beer-and-lemon soda, a *Diesel* mixes beer and cola, and a *Nährbier* ("Near Beer") is low-alcohol lager.

The Best Places: For the classic cliché, nothing beats the rowdy Hofbräuhaus—the only beer hall where you'll actually find oompah music. Locals prefer beer gardens: try the Augustiner (near the train station), the Viktualienmarkt, or the English Garden. All three are listed later in this chapter. If you're in Munich in September through October, you can visit the biggest beer garden of them all—Oktoberfest. If you've had enough fun, beer-hall toilets come with a vomitorium.

Traditional Bavarian Cuisine

Traditional Bavarian cooking is heavy, hearty, fatty, and starchy. Pork dishes served with a side of sauerkraut, dumplings, or potatoes are the norm. These days, however, health-conscious Germans are turning to lighter fare and organic "*Bio*" foods, and German chefs are adopting international influences to jazz up "Modern German" cuisine.

Main Dishes: The classic staple across Germany is sausage—hundreds of varieties of wursts, served with a roll or with sauerkraut as an excuse for a vegetable. Other common dishes are schnitzel—a breaded veal or pork cutlet—and pork knuckle *(Schweinshax'n)*. A dish described as *braten* means "roasted"—as in *Schweinebraten* (roasted pork), or *Bratwurst* (grilled sausage). For a meal-sized salad, order a *Salatteller*.

Besides these foods found all over Germany, there are some Bavarian specialties: *Dampfnudel* is a steamed bread roll with toppings, served as either a savory main dish or sweet dessert. A *Fleischpfanzer* is a big meatball. *Steckerlfisch* is whole mackerel grilled on a stick.

Sides: Common side dishes include *Knödel* (dumplings), *Spätzle* (little noodles), potatoes, soups, and salads. *Spargel* (giant white asparagus) is a must in May-June. Germans make excellent salads—a *grüner*

Fat, starch, nothing fancy—Bavarian cuisine

Pretzel, Weisswurst, beer—a Munich brunch

Salat (mostly lettuce) or *gemischter Salat* (lettuce and mixed vegetables), *Kartoffelsalat* (potato salad), or many more options. Along with their beer, Bavarians enjoy a *Brez'n* (a pretzel) or a *Radi*—a radish that's thinly spiral-cut and salted.

Drinks: Germans love their white wine. Good-quality wines are often available by the glass or quarter-liter (a *Viertel*, 8 oz.). If you order "*Ein Viertel Weisswein, bitte—trocken*" you'll get a large glass of white wine that's "*trocken*"—dry. *Halbtrocken* is medium, and *süss* is sweet. In summer, locals enjoy a refreshing *Weinschorle*—a spritzer of wine with sparkling water. In winter, there's a popular hot-spiced, red-wine punch called *Glühwein*.

The most popular German wines come from the Rhine and Mosel river valleys, not from southern Bavaria. Common grape varieties are *Riesling* (fruity, fragrant, elegant), *Gewürztraminer* ("spicy"), *Müller-Thurgau* (best when young), and *Liebfraumilch* ("beloved maiden's milk," a semi-sweet blending of varieties). From the region of Franconia (north of Munich) comes *Grüner Silvaner,* an acidic, fruity white in a jug-shaped bottle. Germany is not known for its reds, but there's the velvety *Dornfelder* and the pinot noir-like *Spätburgunder*.

Germans enjoy informal take-out stands and beer gardens, where you can order from various vendors.

Eating

Large beer halls often have various dining options—indoor, outdoor, formal waiters, or self-service.

Even teetotalers can enjoy good-quality beers that are non-alcohol ("alkoholfrei"): lagers, Weissbier (wheat-based), or Malztrunk—the sweet, dark, malted beverage that children quaff before they start drinking the real thing. Local soft drinks include spritz drinks like Apfelschorle (apple juice and sparkling water) and Spezi (cola and orange soda).

For coffee, you'll find many of the same drinks (espresso, cappuccino) served in American or Italian coffee shops.

Dessert: While you're sure to have Apfelstrudel (apple-pie filling wrapped in wafer-thin pastry), Germany offers much more. At a bakery (Bäckerei) or pastry shop (Konditorei) you'll find plenty of pastries, often with some kind of filling, like the Krapfen, a Bavarian jelly-filled doughnut. Gummi Bears are local gumdrops with a cult following (look for the Haribo brand). Ice-cream stores, often run by Italian immigrants, abound. Get eine Kugel—a scoop—of your favorite, and stroll the streets. Or join the Germans who enjoy sitting down with fancy sundaes in big bowls.

Guten Appetit!

ON AND NEAR MARIENPLATZ: All these are within a five-minute walk of the main square. S-Bahn Marienplatz.

①	**$$$ Ratskeller** Marienplatz 8, tel. 089/219-9890 www.ratskeller.com	New Town Hall's vast elegant cellar and 360-degree-view courtyard, touristy but has locals too, lunch specials (daily 10:00-24:00)
②	**$ Kantine im Rathaus** In New Town Hall (Enter under glockenspiel and look right for sign)	Fast, no-nonsense cafeteria in New Town Hall courtyard (Mon-Fri 11:00-18:30, Sat 12:00-16:00, closes 17:00 weekdays Jan-April, closed Sun)
③	**$$$ Glockenspiel Café** Marienplatz 28, tel. 089/264-256	Great view over Marienplatz, OK food or just coffee, enter on Rosenstrasse (Mon-Sat 9:00-24:00, Sun 9:00-19:00)
④	**$ Hugendubel Bookstore Café** Marienplatz 22 tel. 089/2601-1987	Self-serve Starbucks-style café on top floor with great view over Marienplatz (Mon-Sat 9:30-20:00, closed Sun; may close—call ahead)
⑤	**$ Der Kleine Chinese** Im Tal 28, tel. 089/2916-3536	Popular Asian standards, order at counter they bring it to you (daily 11:00-22:00)
⑥	**$$ Blatt Salate** Schäfflerstrasse 7, tel. 089/2102-0281	Self-serve salad bar, vegetarian and meat salads, soups, bread, quiet hideaway (Mon-Sat 11:00-19:00, closed Sun)
⑦	**$ Kaufhof** At Marienplatz, Kaufingerstrasse 1	Department store with grocery section for picnic shopping (Mon-Sat 9:30-20:00, closed Sun)

AROUND THE VIKTUALIENMARKT: Colorful market a few steps south of Marienplatz.

⑧	**$ Viktualienmarkt Beer Garden** By the maypole in the center of the market	Buy from surrounding stalls, can eat at beer garden tables (with no tablecloths) with beer purchase from counter (Mon-Sat until late, closed Sun)
⑨	**$ Restaurant Opatija** Enter at Viktualienmarkt 6 tel. 089/2323-1995	Modern and efficient; pizza, pasta, salads, and traditional German cuisine; eat indoors, in quiet courtyard, or takeout (daily 11:30-22:30)

Eating

⑩	**$ Die Münchner Suppenküche** Reichenbachstrasse and Frauenstrasse tel. 089/260-9599	Self-service soup joint with a few picnic tables under a closed-in awning (Mon-Sat 9:00-18:00, closed Sun)
⑪	**$ Stadt Café** At Munich City Museum St.-Jakobs-Platz 1 tel. 089/266-949	Lively, informal, and no-frills; healthy fare—Italian, German, vegetarian, salads, cake-by-the-slice; daily specials (daily 10:00-24:00)
⑫	**$$$ Prinz Myshkin Vegetarian Restaurant** Hackenstrasse 2 tel. 089/265-596	Upscale vegetarian (pastas, Indian dishes); modern inside or quiet outside; appetizer buffet, weekday lunch specials (daily 11:30-23:00)
⑬	**$ Sebastiansplatz Eateries** On Sebastiansplatz	Many interesting bistros line this cobbled square—French, Italian, Asian, salad places; nearby Schrannenhalle has more options (Mon-Sat 10:00-20:00)
⑭	**$$$ Der Pschorr** Viktualienmarkt 15 tel. 089/442-383-940 www.der-pschorr.de	Upscale beer hall with view terrace over Viktualienmarkt, arguably Munich's finest beer, organic "slow food" mixes mod and trad, lunch specials (daily 10:00-24:00)

ELSEWHERE IN THE OLD TOWN: Most of these are within a 10-minute walk of Marienplatz.

⑮	**$$ Hofbräuhaus** Platzl 9 tel. 089/2901-3610 www.hofbraeuhaus.de	World's most famous beer hall, grotesquely touristy but fun, oompah band; best for beer and wurst, but the food's good; seating areas from rowdy to mellow, upstairs has free folk shows (daily 9:00-23:30)
⑯	**$$$ Wirtshaus Ayingers** Platzl 1a	tel. 089/2370-3666	www.ayingers.de	Quieter neighbor of Hofbräuhaus, quality schnitzels and beer, lively outside or woody interior (daily 11:00-23:30)
⑰	**$$$ Haxnbauer** Sparkassenstrasse 6 tel. 089/216-6540	Stark old elegant place where locals come for best pork knuckle (*Schweinshaxe*) in town (daily 11:00-23:00)

⑱	**$$ Jodlerwirt** Altenhofstrasse 4 tel. 089/221-249 | www. jodlerwirt-muenchen.net	Cramped, smart-alecky pub with great food, accordion music and fun Bavarian ambience (Tue-Sat 19:00-23:00 or later, closed Sun-Mon)
⑲	**$$ Andechser am Dom** Weinstrasse 7a tel. 089/2429-2920 | www. andechser-am-dom.de	Behind the Frauenkirche, trendy place with Andechs beer, great food, and regulars; *Gourmetteller* sampler plate; reserve during peak times (daily 10:00-24:00)
⑳	**$$ Nürnberger Bratwurst Glöckl am Dom** Frauenplatz 9 tel. 089/291-9450 www.bratwurst-gloeckl.de	Traditional Bavarian atmosphere (and tourists), outside under trees or dark medieval interior, Nürnberger sausages (daily 10:00-24:00)
㉑	**$$ Altes Hackerhaus** Sendlinger Strasse 14 tel. 089/260-5026 www.hackerhaus.de	Traditional Bavarian food (and locals), slightly fancy; historic building with courtyard or interior nooks; Hacker-Pschorr beer (daily 10:00-24:00)
㉒	**$$$ Spatenhaus** Residenzstrasse 12 tel. 089/290-7050 www.spatenhaus.de	The operagoers' beer hall, top-notch Bavarian cuisine in elegant woodsy setting, or outside, or upstairs—where reservations are smart (daily 9:30-24:00)
㉓	**$$$ Brenner Grill** Maximilianstrasse 15 tel. 089/452-2880	Steak, fish, and international dishes served under a forest of pillars (long hours daily)
㉔	**$$ Café Luitpold** Brienner Strasse 11 tel. 089/242-8750	Where Munich's high society comes for coffee and their signature sponge cake (Mon 8:00-19:00, Tue-Sat 8:00-23:00, Sun 9:00-19:00)
㉕	**$$ Dallmayr Delicatessen** Dienerstrasse 13-15 tel. 089/213-5110	Gourmet foods for take-out picnics, or pricey cafés for light meals—for more info see page 31 (Mon-Sat 9:30-19:00, closed Sun)

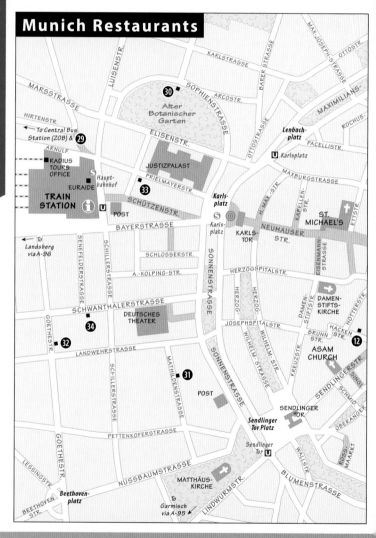

Munich Restaurants

KARLSTRASSE

SOPHIENSTRASSE

MARSSTRASSE

HIRTENSTR.

← To Central Bus Station (ZOB) & 29

Alter Botanischer Garten

30

LUISENSTR.

ELISENSTR.

Lenbach-platz

U Karlsplatz

PACELLISTR.

ARNULF

RADIUS TOURS OFFICE

EURAIDE

Haupt-bahnhof

JUSTIZPALAST

MAXBURGSTRASSE

TRAIN STATION

33

PRIELMAYERSTR.

Karls-platz

ST. MICHAEL'S

U

SCHÜTZENSTR.

POST

Karls-platz

KARLS-TOR

NEUHAUSER STR.

← To Landsberg via A-96

BAYERSTRASSE

SCHLOSSERSTR.

A.-KOLPING-STR.

HERZOGSPITALSTR.

DAMEN-STIFTS-KIRCHE

SCHWANTHALERSTRASSE

34

DEUTSCHES THEATER

JOSEPHSPITALSTR.

32

LANDWEHRSTRASSE

ASAM CHURCH

12

31

POST

SENDLINGER TOR

PETTENKOFERSTRASSE

Sendlinger Tor Platz

Sendlinger Tor U

NUSSBAUMSTRASSE

MATTHÄUS-KIRCHE

BLUMENSTRASSE

Beethoven-platz

← To Garmisch via A-95

LINDWURMSTR.

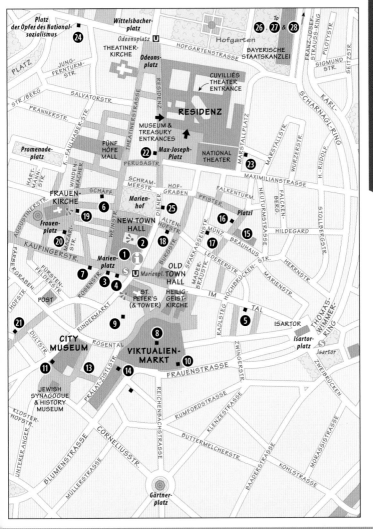

IN THE ENGLISH GARDEN: Outdoor ambience in sprawling public park. Most places are a 10-minute walk from any tram or U-Bahn stop.

26	**$ Chinese Tower Beer Garden** By the Chinese Tower tel. 089/383-8730 www.chinaturm.de	6,000 seats under the sky, usually live music, buy food from stalls (try the Steckerlfisch) or bring your own (daily, long hours in good weather)
27	**$$$ Seehaus** Kleinhesselohe 3 tel. 089/381-6130	Dressy and snobbish, locals love idyllic lakeside setting or classy indoors, excellent Mediterranean and traditional fare (daily 10:00-24:00)
28	**$$ Seehaus Beer Garden** Kleinhesselohe 3 tel. 089/381-6130	Same lakeside setting, more casual, traditional beer-hall fare (daily, long hours from 11:00)

NEAR THE TRAIN STATION: Less atmospheric neighborhood, but some good bargains and local feel.

29	**$$ Augustiner Beer Garden** Arnulfstrasse 52 tel. 089/594-393 www.augustinerkeller.de	Possibly Munich's best beer garden, sprawling under-the-leaves haven for locals on balmy evening, traditional foods, self-service or table-service restaurants (daily 11:00-24:00)
30	**$$ Park Café** Sophienstrasse 7 tel. 089/5161-7980 www.parkcafe089.de	Beer garden with big and bold indoor section or pleasant outdoors (either self-service or menu), few tourists, quality food (daily 11:00-24:00)
31	**$$ La Vecchia Masseria** Mathildenstrasse 3 tel. 089/550-9090	Italian food in cozy Tuscan interior or flowery courtyard, €25 fixed-price *menu*, reservations smart (daily 11:30-23:30)
32	**$ Altin Dilim** Goethestrasse 17 tel. 089/9734-0869	Cafeteria-style authentic Turkish food, large selection, ample seating, easy to order, pay at counter (Mon-Sat 7:00-24:00, Sun 10:00-24:00)
33	**$ Karstadt Department Store** Bahnhofplatz 7	Grocery section good for picnic shopping (Mon-Sat 9:30-20:00, closed Sun)
34	**$ Lidl** Schwanthalerstrasse 31	Multi-purpose store with groceries for picnic shopping (Mon-Sat 8:00-20:00, closed Sun)

Neuschwanstein Castle and a Bit of Bavaria

Europe's most spectacular castle (and that's really saying something!) lies 80 miles southwest of Munich. Perched dramatically on a hill, with its proud white turrets, it's impressive outside and luxurious inside.

This chapter focuses on seeing Neuschwanstein Castle (noy-SHVAHN-stine) on a day trip from Munich, either on your own or with a tour. I also cover other nearby options: You could fit in a visit to the equally historic Hohenschwangau Castle (located within sight of Neuschwanstein), take short hikes with great alpine scenery, and see a few other sights near the King's Castles area. Advance reservations for Neuschwanstein are a magic wand that can smooth out your visit.

With more time (and, ideally, a rental car), stay overnight in the nearby town of Füssen and explore more of Bavaria—a picturesque land of cute villages, painted buildings shared by cows and farmers, and locals who still dress in dirndls and lederhosen and yodel when they're happy.

ORIENTATION TO NEUSCHWANSTEIN CASTLE

Cost: €13, includes (required) timed-entry, English-language tour. The €25 "Königsticket" combo-ticket includes Hohenschwangau Castle (described on page 126). Entry is free for kids under 18 (with adult).

Hours: The Neuschwanstein and Hohenschwangau ticket center is open daily (April-Sept 8:00-17:00, Oct-March 9:00-15:00). The first castle tour of the day departs an hour after the ticket center opens and the last normally departs 30 minutes after it closes: April-Sept at 9:00 and 17:30, Oct-March at 10:00 and 15:30.

Reservations: It's smart to reserve at least a day ahead for April through October, and a week ahead in July and August. Reservations cost

Reservations for Neuschwanstein are smart. Order ahead, then pick up your timed-entry ticket there.

€1.80 per ticket and must be made online at least two days in advance (no later than 15:00 local time, www.hohenschwangau.de). With notice, a few hotels can book tickets for you. When you arrive at Neuschwanstein, go to the ticket center (in the village between the two castles) to pick up your reserved tickets an hour before the appointed entry time. If you're late, you may have to re-book for a later slot.

Buying Tickets on the Spot: Buy tickets at the ticket center located in the village between the two castles. Your ticket will come with a reserved entry time. This can be as little as one hour after purchase, or (in the crowds of summer) many hours later. Don't assume you can buy a ticket right at closing time—afternoon tours can sell out.

Avoiding Crowds: In summer, it's very crowded from 10:00 to 14:00. So either make a reservation, or arrive as early as possible to buy tickets (ideally, right at 8:00), or visit at 14:00 (to get a late-afternoon entry).

Getting There: For details on reaching the castle from Munich with a guided tour, via public transportation, or with a rental car, see "Getting to Neuschwanstein Castle," later.

Seeing Hohenschwangau Castle: To tour both castles, you're required to do Hohenschwangau first. You'll get two tour times: Hohenschwangau and then, two hours later, Neuschwanstein.

Tourist Services in the Village of Hohenschwangau: The village TI (run by helpful Thomas) is open daily (April-Sept 10:00-17:30, Oct-March 10:00-16:00, tel. 08362/819-765, www.schwangau.de). You'll also find an ATM, WC (€0.50), lockers (€1), coin-op Internet terminal, and telephones.

Eating: The village restaurants are mediocre and overpriced. I enjoy a picnic alongside the picturesque Alpsee (the nearby lake)—but you'll need to bring your own picnic from Munich or Füssen (there are no grocery stores here), or get a take-out sandwich or bratwurst. For a hot meal, the yellow Bräustüberl cafeteria (€6-7 grill meals) won't be the highlight of your visit. Up the hill near Neuschwanstein Castle is another cluster of overpriced eateries. A small cafeteria is inside the castle, at the end of your guided tour.

Getting To Neuschwanstein Castle

The castle and nearby sights are two hours from Munich by train or car. The easiest way to see the castle is by booking a guided tour: It gets you there and back in a single day, and includes an English-speaking guide and a reserved castle entry. But Neuschwanstein is also completely doable on your own. Here are your options:

By Guided Tour: Gray Line Tours offers an all-day bus tour (in both German and English) that includes Neuschwanstein, plus the exquisite Linderhof Castle and the cute wood-carving town of Oberammergau. Those extras are nice, but it also makes for a rushed day. Tours meet at 8:10 at the Karstadt department store across from the Munich train station (€51 plus €23 more for the two castle admissions, daily all year, advisable to book a day in advance in summer, www.sightseeing-munich.com).

Bus Bavaria (run by Mike's Bike Tours) is an all-English bus tour that includes Neuschwanstein plus a scenic bike ride and short hike. Groups meet near the Hofbräuhaus at Bräuhausstrasse 10 (€59, plus €12 castle admission; June-mid-Aug Mon-Tue and Thu-Sat; less frequent May and mid-Aug-Oktoberfest; daily during Oktoberfest; check web for departure times, tel. 089/2554-3987, mobile 0172-852-0660, advisable to book a day in advance in summer, www.mikesbiketours.com).

Radius Tours runs all-day tours to Neuschwanstein using public transportation. Your guide escorts you onto the train to Füssen and then the bus from there to the castle, gives you some general information, and helps you into the castle for the standard tour. Groups depart at 9:30 from the Munich train station near track 32 and are back by 19:00 (€39, plus €12 castle admission; daily April-Dec; Jan-March tours run Mon, Wed, and Fri-Sun; confirm times when you reserve, book a day in advance in summer, www.radiustours.com).

On Your Own by Public Transportation: This surprisingly easy trip involves a two-hour train ride to Füssen, then a short bus trip to Neuschwanstein, where you buy your ticket or pick up your reserved ticket. If you have a reservation, you'll want to leave Munich four hours before your assigned entry time. Here's a typical itinerary:

7:53—Catch train from Munich to Füssen. Trains leave hourly (usually at :53 past the hour), take just over two hours, and most require an (easy) transfer in Kaufbeuren.

10:00—Arrive in Füssen, two miles from Neuschwanstein. At the train station, catch bus #73 or #78 to Neuschwanstein. Buses leave hourly, usually at :05 past the hour (€2.10 each way, 10 minutes). Alternatively, you could take a taxi (€10 one-way), ride a rental bike (2 level miles—see "Bike Rental" on page 129), or even walk (less than an hour).

10:30—Arrive at the base of Neuschwanstein Castle. The bus drops you off in the village of Hohenschwangau, right by the ticket center and TI. Buy your ticket (or confirm your reservation), and start making your way up the hill to the castle entrance (see "Arrival at Neuschwanstein" on page 120).

12:00—Tour Neuschwanstein Castle.

13:00—You're free to do more sightseeing in the area (using my suggestions) or start making your way back to Munich (which is at least 3 hours away from this point).

If you can postpone leaving Munich until after 9:00 on weekday mornings, the **Regional Day Ticket for Bavaria** pass is a great deal, especially for small groups. It covers the train to Füssen, the bus to Neuschwanstein, and more (€25/day for the first person plus €6 for each additional person; the **Schönes-Wochenende-Ticket** is a similar weekend version; for details see "regional tickets" at www.bahn.com).

By Rental Car: It's best to reserve a rental car before your trip, but there are car-rental agencies in the Munich train station (upstairs opposite track 21) and near Füssen (closed Sun—see page 129). From Munich, drive two hours on the A-96 to Füssen, then follow signs to *Königsschlösser*. Once at Neuschwanstein, the most convenient parking lot is #4, *Parkplatz am Alpsee* (€5).

King's Castles Area

Forggensee

BOAT RENTAL

400 Meters
400 Yards

To
Munich
via
Kaufbeuren

SCHELLEWEG
FRAUENBERGSTR.

Füssen

KUPPRECHT-STRASSE
AUGSBURGER STRASSE
THERESIENSTRASSE

VON-FREYBERG-STR.
To
Car Rental

TRAIN STATION

(P-5)
SHOPPING MALL

Horn

#73 & 78 B
SEBASTIANSTR.

KEMPTENER STR.

HIGH CASTLE

(P-3)

HERITAGE MUSEUM

FRANCISCAN MONASTERY

FORCHENWEG
AM LECHRAIN

ALATSEESTR.
BENEDICTINE MONASTERY
SCHWANGAUER STR.
17

TIROLER STR.

Lech Falls

KID-FRIENDLY PARK
NATURE CENTER

Ziegelwies
B
TREETOP WALKWAY

Lech River

Schwansee

P
17

To
Reutte, Austria

GERMANY

AUSTRIA

Alpsee

🐎 Horse Carriage Stops

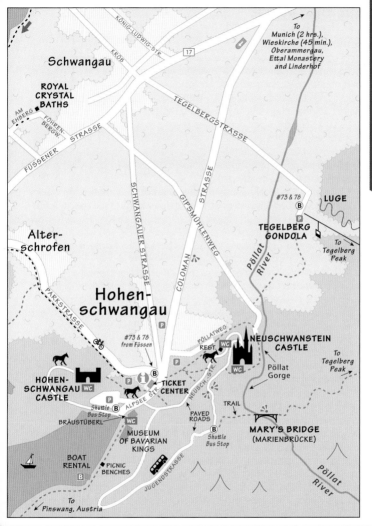

KÖNIG-LUDWIG-STR.

KRÖB

17

To
Munich (2 hrs.),
Wieskirche (45 min.),
Oberammergau,
Ettal Monastery
and Linderhof

Schwangau

ROYAL
CRYSTAL
BATHS

AM EHBERG

FÖHREN-BERGW.

FÜSSENER STRASSE

TEGELBERGSTRASSE

GIPSMÜHLENWEG

STRASSE

SCHWANGAUER STRASSE

COLOMAN

Pöllat River

#73 & 78

LUGE

TEGELBERG
GONDOLA

To
Tegelberg
Peak

Alter-
schrofen

Hohen-
schwangau

PARKSTRASSE

#73 & 78
from Füssen

P

P

POLLATWEG

REST.

WC

NEUSCHWANSTEIN
CASTLE

WC

Pöllat
Gorge

To
Tegelberg
Peak

HOHEN-
SCHWANGAU
CASTLE

WC

ALPSEE STR.

NEUSCH.-STR.

Shuttle
Bus Stop

B

BRÄUSTÜBERL

WC

TICKET
CENTER

P

B

MUSEUM
OF BAVARIAN
KINGS

PAVED
ROADS

TRAIL

B

Shuttle
Bus Stop

MARY'S BRIDGE
(MARIENBRÜCKE)

Pöllat
River

BOAT
RENTAL

B

PICNIC
BENCHES

JUGENDSTRASSE

To
Pinswang, Austria

THE TOUR BEGINS

Arrival at Neuschwanstein

You arrive (by bus, car, taxi, or bike) in the tiny village called Hohenschwangau (hoh-en-SHVAHN-gow). You immediately see the two castles a half-mile apart: yellow Hohenschwangau Castle on a small hill, and ghostly white Neuschwanstein higher up and farther off. In the valley between sits the village and its tourist services, beside a pristine alpine lake. It's easy to find the ticket center, where you can buy castle tickets or pick up your reserved tickets. (If you're fitting Hohenschwangau Castle into your visit, remember that you're required to see that sight first—see page 126.) Once you have your ticket and entry time squared away, start making your way up the hill to the white castle.

Getting Up to Neuschwanstein Castle: It's a moderately steep, 30-minute **walk** up a paved road, through the woods to the castle. A **bus** (€1.80 one-way) leaves every 20 minutes from the parking lot just below Hohenschwengau, stopping at Mary's Bridge, leaving you with a 10-minute *downhill* walk to the castle. The romantic-but-slow **horse-drawn carriages** (€6) drop you to within a five-minute uphill walk to the castle. Both conveyances can have long lines at peak times. I enjoy the walk.

▶ *Once at the castle doors, wait at the entry for your ticket number to light up on the board. When your entry time appears, don't be shy—power through the milling crowds, insert your ticket in the turnstile, and pass through. Be on time. If you miss your entry window, you will not be allowed in. Inside, you're met by your (required) guide, who leads you and 59 others on an interesting—if rushed—30-minute tour.*

Castle Exterior

Imagine "Mad" King Ludwig as a boy, climbing the hills above his dad's castle, Hohenschwangau, dreaming up the ultimate fairy-tale castle. Inheriting the throne at the young age of 18, he had the power to make his dream concrete and stucco. Neuschwanstein (roughly "New Swanstone") was designed first by a theater-set designer...then by an architect. While it was built upon the ruins of an old castle and looks medieval, Neuschwanstein is modern iron-and-brick construction with a sandstone veneer—only about as old as the Eiffel Tower. It feels like something you'd see at a home show for 19th-century royalty. Built from 1869 to 1886, it's the epitome of the Romanticism popular in 19th-century Europe. Construction stopped with

Neuschwanstein Castle looks medieval but is only 150 years old and has modern conveniences.

"Mad" King Ludwig (1845-1886)

A tragic figure, Ludwig II (a.k.a. "Mad" King Ludwig) ruled Bavaria for 22 years until his death in 1886 at the age of 40. Bavaria was weak. Politically, Ludwig's reality was to "rule" either as a pawn of Prussia or a pawn of Austria. Rather than deal with politics in Bavaria's capital, Munich, Ludwig frittered away most of his time at his family's hunting palace, Hohenschwangau. He spent much of his adult life constructing his fanciful Neuschwanstein Castle—like a kid builds a tree house—on a neighboring hill upon the scant ruins of a medieval castle. Here and in his other projects (Linderhof Castle and the unrealized Falkenstein Castle), even as he strove to evoke medieval grandeur, Ludwig embraced the state-of-the-art technology of the Industrial Age in which he lived. Neuschwanstein had electricity, running water, and a telephone (but no Wi-Fi).

Ludwig was a true romantic living in a Romantic age. His best friends were artists, poets, and composers such as Richard Wagner. His palaces are wallpapered with misty medieval themes—especially those from Wagnerian operas.

Although Ludwig spent 17 years building Neuschwanstein, he lived in it only 172 days. Soon after he moved in (and before his vision for the castle was completed), Ludwig was declared mentally unfit to rule Bavaria and taken away. Two days after this eviction, Ludwig was found dead in a lake. To this day, people debate whether the king was murdered or committed suicide.

Ludwig's death (only a third of the interior was finished), and within six weeks, tourists were paying to go through it.

During World War II, the Nazis used Neuschwanstein as one of their primary secret storehouses for stolen art. At war's end, the art was discovered and saved by the Allied company known as the "Monuments Men."

Inside the Castle—The Guided Visit

Once inside, your guide will lead you up and down more than 300 steps, visiting 15 lavish rooms with their original furnishings and fanciful wall paintings—mostly based on Wagnerian opera themes.

Ludwig's extravagant **throne room,** modeled in a Neo-Byzantine style to emphasize his royal status, celebrates six valiant Christian kings (whose mantle Ludwig clearly believed he had donned) under a huge gilded-bronze chandelier. The exquisite two-million-stone mosaic floor is a visual encyclopedia of animals and plant life. The most memorable stop may be the king's gilded-lily **bedroom,** with his elaborately carved canopy bed (with a forest of Gothic church spires on top), washstand (filled with water piped in from the Alps), and personal chapel. After passing through Ludwig's **living room** (decorated with more than 150 swans) and a faux **grotto,** you'll climb to the fourth floor for the grand finale: the **Singers' Hall,** an ornately decorated space filled with murals depicting the story of Parzival, the legendary medieval figure with whom Ludwig identified.

After the Guided Tour—More Castle Exhibits

After your guide says *Auf Wiedersehen,* you still have a few more rooms on your own. Spend 13 minutes with the informative video on how the castle was built. It also brings to life all of the unfinished parts of

The throne room—Neo-Byzantine mosaics

Singers' Hall, where Wagner operas played

Ludwig's vision—more prickly towers, a central chapel, a fancy view terrace, an ornate bathhouse, and more. Finally you'll see a digital model of Falkenstein—a never-built castle that occupied Ludwig's unbounded fantasies the year he died.

Next comes the kitchen—state-of-the-art for this high-tech king in its day. Then you'll see a room lined with fascinating drawings of the castle plans, as well as a large castle model. After the obligatory gift shop (and some rare WCs you should consider using), you'll spill back outside.

▶ *If you're ready to head **back to the village,** turn right to return on foot or take a horse-drawn carriage ride (only €3 going down), or turn left to catch the bus (following signs toward Mary's Bridge).*

*Or, to **continue this tour,** adding about 40 minutes more to your visit, turn left to see Mary's Bridge (a 10-minute uphill hike) and then return to the village via the scenic Pöllat Gorge.*

Mary's Bridge (Marienbrücke)

As you hike the trail up to the bridge, you get scenic glimpses back on Neuschwanstein's facade in one direction, and classic views of

Mary's Bridge—dramatically spanning the Pöllat Gorge—has postcard views back at the castle.

Hohenschwangau in the other. You'll also pass the stop for the bus back to the village.

Finally, you arrive at Mary's Bridge. This narrow pedestrian bridge over a cavernous gorge gives you a postcard view of Neuschwanstein and the lake in the distance. Jockey with a United Nations of tourists for the best angle. Marvel at Ludwig's castle, just as Ludwig did. This bridge was quite an engineering accomplishment 100 years ago.

▶ *Now let's return to the village by way of a meandering downhill trail through the Pöllat Gorge beneath you. Start backtracking toward Neuschwanstein, while keeping an eye out for the trailhead (look for Pöllatschlucht signs). The trail starts with a series of concrete stairs. The trail is not dangerous or taxing, but it can be slippery, and is closed in winter. (If you're not up for the hike, take the bus back.)*

Pöllat Gorge Walk (Pöllatschlucht)

The river gorge that slices into the rock just behind Neuschwanstein's lofty perch is a more scenic and less crowded alternative to shuffling back down the main road. It only takes about 15 minutes more.

Descend the stairs, with Germany's finest castle looming through the trees. You'll pop out along the Pöllat River, passing a little beach (with neatly stacked stones) offering a view up at the grand waterfall that gushes beneath Mary's Bridge. From here, follow the river as it goes over several smaller waterfalls, strolling along steel walkways and railings that help make this slippery area safer. After passing an old wooden channel used to harness the power of all that water, you'll hit level ground.

▶ *Back on the valley floor, turn left (when you can) and walk through a pleasantly untouristy residential area to return to the village.*

MORE SIGHTS NEAR NEUSCHWANSTEIN CASTLE

With more time, consider these sights. The first three are right at the village of Hohenschwangau. The Tegelberg gondola and luge are a short bus, bike, or car ride (or 30-minute walk) away. The main sight to see is clearly Hohenschwangau Castle.

▲▲▲Hohenschwangau Castle

Standing quietly below Neuschwanstein, the big, yellow Hohenschwangau Castle was Ludwig's boyhood home. Originally built in the 12th century, it was ruined by Napoleon. Ludwig's father, King Maximilian II, rebuilt it in 1830. Hohenschwangau (loosely translated as "High Swanland") was used by the royal family as a summer hunting lodge until 1912. The Wittelsbach family (which ruled Bavaria for nearly seven centuries) still owns the place (and lived in the annex—today's shop—until the 1970s).

The required 30-minute tours are excellent, giving a better glimpse of Ludwig's life than the more-visited and famous Neuschwanstein Castle tour. Tours here are smaller (35 people rather than 60) and more relaxed.

The interior decor (mostly Neo-Gothic, like the castle itself) is harmonious, cohesive, and original—all done in 1835, with paintings inspired by Romantic themes. As you tour the castle, imagine how the paintings must have inspired young Ludwig. For 17 years, he lived here at his dad's place and followed the construction of his dream castle across the way—you'll see the telescope still set up and directed at Neuschwanstein.

You'll explore rooms on two floors—the queen's rooms, and then, upstairs, the king's. (Conveniently, their bedrooms were connected by a secret passage.) You'll see photos and busts of Ludwig and his little brother, Otto; some Turkish-style flourishes (to please the king, who had been impressed after a visit to the Orient); more than 25 different depictions of swans (honoring the Knights of Schwangau, whose legacy the Wittelsbachs inherited); over-the-top gifts the Wittelsbachs received from their adoring subjects; and paintings of VIGs (very important Germans, including Martin Luther—who may or may not have visited here—and an infant Charlemagne).

One of the most impressive rooms is the Banquet Hall (also known as the Hall of Heroes); one vivid wall mural depicts a savage, yet bloodless, fifth-century barbarian battle. You'll also see Ludwig's bedroom, which he

Hohenschwangau, Ludwig's boyhood home

There's winners and lugers, but fun for all.

inherited from his father. He kept most of the decor (including the nude nymphs frolicking over his bed), but painted the ceiling black and installed transparent stars that could be lit from the floor above to create the illusion of a night sky.

▶ *€12 timed-entry ticket, includes required guided tour. €23 combo-ticket with Neuschwanstein Castle. Hohenswangau's hours and ticket-buying procedure are the same as for Neuschwanstein—see page 115. If visiting both castles, you're required to visit Hohenschwangau before Neuschwanstein.*

Museum of the Bavarian Kings (Museum der Bayerischen Könige)

This museum is overpriced and skippable, but it's well-presented in a former grand hotel on the shore of the Alpsee, and nice for killing time on a rainy day. It documents the history of the royal Wittelsbachs with portraits, busts, an impressive dining set, and Ludwig II's outlandish royal robe and fairy-tale sword.

▶ *€11, combo-tickets available with the castles; daily April-Sept 9:00-19:00, Oct-March 10:00-18:00; includes dry audioguide, Alpseestrasse 27, tel. 08362/926-4640, www.museumderbayerischenkoenige.de.*

Alpsee

The scenic lake next to the village makes for a pleasant picnic or an easy 1.5-hour walking loop (some stairs). In summer, they rent boats from the dock on the left bank, 200 yards down.

▲Tegelberg Gondola (Tegelbergbahn) and Luge (Sommerrodelbahn)

Two fun sights cluster a couple of miles north of Neuschwanstein—an easy bus or bike ride away.

The gondola (cable car) is a five-minute ride up to the mountain's 5,500-foot summit, with great views of the Alps and of hang gliders and paragliders leaping into airborne ecstasy.

The summer luge course is like a bobsled on wheels. A funky cable system pulls you and your sled up to the top, where you whiz down the hill along a metal track. You control the brake to go as slow or fast as you want. You'll reach the bottom with a wind-blown hairdo and smile-creased face—and want to go right back up.

There's also a playground, a cheery eatery, and even the stubby remains of an ancient Roman villa.

▶ *In bad weather, the gondola and/or luge may not run at all, and in good weather hours may be longer—call to confirm. Gondola—€19 round-trip, daily 9:00 until last descent at 17:00 (April-Oct) or 16:00 (mid-Dec-March), closed Nov-mid-Dec. Luge—€3.50/ride, shareable 6-ride card-€15; hours vary but typically July-Sept daily 10:00-18:00; April-June Mon-Fri 13:00-17:00, Sat-Sun 10:00-17:00; waits can be long in good weather, children under 8 must ride with adult, tel. 08362/98360, www. tegelbergbahn.de.*

__Getting There:__ It's a 30-minute walk or 10-minute bike ride from the town of Hohenschwangau. Or catch bus #73 or #78.

FÜSSEN

The charming town of Füssen (FEW-sehn)—three miles west of Neuschwanstein—is the handiest overnight base for exploring the area. Dramatically situated under a castle on the lively Lech River, it's historic and cobbled-cutesy. It has a range of good hotels and restaurants, and some worthwhile sights. Everything I mention is walking distance in this small town, but renting a bike is a great way to get around.

Orientation to Füssen

Arrival: The Füssen train station is your transportation hub. Trains connect to Munich (hourly departures, 2 hours, some trains to Munich change

One Full Day at Neuschwanstein

If you have all day to see Neuschwanstein Castle and its nearby sights, here's a possible day plan:

8:00—Arrive in the village of Hohenschwangau. Buy tickets or pick up reserved tickets.

9:00—Visit Hohenschwangau Castle with the guided tour.

10:00—Hike, bus, or clip-clop up to Neuschwanstein, and wait for your entry time.

11:00—Tour Neuschwanstein Castle with the guided tour.

12:00—Hike up to Mary's Bridge for great views, then descend by way of the scenic Pöllat Gorge.

13:00—Lunch by the Alpsee: Grab a picnic or cheap takeout.

14:00—Bus, bike, or walk to the Tegelberg gondola and luge.

16:00—You're free for more sightseeing around Neuschwanstein or in Füssen (Royal Crystal Baths are open late).

in Buchloe). Also from the train station, you can catch buses to Neuschwanstein (#73 or #78 leave hourly, usually at :05 past the hour, €2.10 each way, 10 minutes). You can also catch a taxi (€10 one-way).

Bike Rental: At the train station, rent bikes at Fahrrad-Station (€10-20 for 24 hours depending on the bike; March-Oct Mon-Fri 9:00-12:00 & 14:00-18:00, Sat 9:00-13:00, Sun 10:00-12:00, closed Nov-Feb; tel. 08362/505-9155, mobile 0176-2205-3080, www.ski-sport-luggi.de).

Helpful Hints: There's a helpful TI near the train station (tel. 08362/93850, www.fuessen.de). A car-rental agency is 1.5 miles west of the station (Schlichtling, closed Sun, Hiebeler Strasse 49, tel. 08362/922-122, www.schlichtling.de). A good local guide with a car is Silvia Beyer (€30/hour, mobile 0160-9011-3431, silliby@web.de). If you're staying overnight, your mandatory hotel tax entitles you to the Füssen Card, which gives you some free bus rides and sightseeing discounts—ask your hotel about it.

Sights in and near Füssen

▲Füssen Heritage Museum

The town's one must-see sight stars the *Dance of Death*. Painted shortly after the devastating 1590 plague, it shows 20 different people from every social class, each dancing with the Grim Reaper. The museum also has some exquisitely decorated old rooms, plus exhibits on violin-making and cloth-making.

▶ €6; April-Oct Tue-Sun 11:00-17:00, closed Mon; shorter hours and closed Mon-Thu Nov-March; tel. 08362/903-146, www.museum. fuessen.de.

▲Royal Crystal Baths (Königliche Kristall-Therme)

A mile east of town is this pool/sauna complex—the perfect way to warm up on a cold day or cool off on a hot one. It has indoor swimming pools and mineral baths downstairs (swimsuits required), and a sauna upstairs (swimsuits forbidden). You can buy (but not rent) swimsuits there. From Füssen, drive, bike, or walk across the river, turn left toward Schwangau, and then (about a mile later) turn left at signs for *Kristall-Therme*.

▶ €11-30, depending on services; daily 9:00-22:00, Fri-Sat until 23:00, nude swimming everywhere Tue and Fri after 19:00; Am Ehberg 16, tel. 08362/819-630, www.kristalltherme-schwangau.de.

▲Bike Rides

This is great biking country. Many hotels loan bikes to guests, or you can rent at the Füssen train station. Biking to **Neuschwanstein** is easy and mostly flat, and you could continue north to the **Tegelberg** gondola and luge.

On a beautiful day, nothing beats a bike ride around the bright-turquoise **Forggensee,** the lake a half-mile north of Füssen. This 20-mile circular ride is mostly flat on paved bike paths, is occasionally strenuous, always scenic, and takes about three hours (including a short stop for a picnic you brought along). From Füssen, head north following *Festspielhaus* signs. Once you reach the theater, follow *Forggensee Rundweg* signs (the circular path around the lake). Locals swear it's easiest to go clockwise.

You can also take one- or two-hour round-trip **boat cruises** on the Forggensee, leaving either from the Füssen "harbor" (*Bootshafen*) or the theater (*Festspielhaus*). You can bring a bike onto the boat (if it's not too

Füssen has charm, location, and services.

Lech Falls, a short walk from town

crowded) and get off across the lake—shortening the total loop (€8, about hourly, runs daily June-mid-Oct, tel. 08362/921-363, www.stadt-fuessen. de—click on "*Forggensee-Schiffahrt*").

Lech Falls and Treetop Walkway (Baumkronenweg Ziegelwies)

Another pleasant walk from town is to head south across the river and turn right (upstream) to Lechfall, a thunderous waterfall.

Another 500 yards farther up the road is a small museum about local flora and fauna. Through the museum, you gain access to a wooden suspension-bridge that lets you walk for a third of a mile among the treetops, actually crossing the German-Austrian border—no passport check (€4, daily May-Oct 10:00-17:00, closed Nov-April and in bad weather, last entry at 16:30, Tiroler Strasse 10, tel. 08362/938-7550, www.baum kronenweg.eu).

Sleeping and Eating in Füssen

All of my recommended accommodations and restaurants are close to the town center. Most hotels give about 5-10 percent off for two-night stays—always request this discount.

Sleeping: These big, fancy hotels are within a few minutes' walk of the train station. **$$$ Hotel Schlosskrone** (Prinzregentenplatz 2-4, tel. 08362/930-180, www.schlosskrone.de). **$$$ Hotel Hirsch** (Kaiser-Maximilian-Platz 7, tel. 08362/93980, www.hotelfuessen.de).

These smaller, mid-priced places are also centrally located. **$$ Altstadthotel zum Hechten** (Ritterstrasse 6, tel. 08362/91600, www.hotel-hechten.com). **$$ Gästehaus Schöberl** (Luitpoldstrasse 14-16, tel. 08362/922-411, www.schoeberl-fuessen.de).

For budget beds, consider **$ Old Kings Design Hostel** (8-bed backpacker dorm rooms and some doubles, Franziskanergasse 2, tel. 08362/883-7385, www.oldkingshostel.com).

Eating: **$$ Restaurant Ritterstub'n** has delicious Bavarian fare, fish, salads, veggie plates, and a kids' menu; eat inside or in the courtyard (Tue-Sun 11:30-14:30 & 17:30-23:00, closed Mon, Ritterstrasse 4, tel. 08362/7759). **$$ Schenke & Wirtshaus** has traditional Bavarian dishes and Lech River pike in a cozy setting (daily 11:00-22:00, Ritterstrasse 6, tel. 0836/91600). **$$$ Ristorante La Perla** offers upscale Italian in a classic interior, a courtyard, or streetside (daily 11:00-22:00, in winter closed 14:30-17:30 and all day Mon, Drehergasse 44, tel. 08362/7155).

For simpler fare, try the **$ food court** at the Markthalle (Schrannengasse 12) or the **$ ethnic food joints** in the Luitpold-Passage (Luitpoldstrasse 1), or buy picnic supplies at **$ Netto Grocery** (Mon-Sat 7:00-20:00, underground at Prinzregentenplatz). **$ Hohes Schloss Italian Ice Cream** is great for *gelato* and people-watching (Reichenstrasse 14).

MORE BAVARIAN SIGHTS

There are many more great Bavarian sights, but most require a rental car... and a different guidebook.

There's the ▲▲ **Wieskirche,** an ornately decorated Baroque church in a humble pasture (www.wieskirche.de). ▲ **Oberammergau** is Germany's woodcarving capital and home of the famous Passion Play (www.ammergauer-alpen.de). **Ettal Monastery** is another fancy church (www.klosterettal.de). ▲▲ **Linderhof,** yet another of Ludwig's castles, is an exquisite mini-Versailles with a palace and gardens set in the woods (www.linderhof.de).

With a rental car, you could see all of these (as well as Neuschwanstein) in a single long day from either Munich or Füssen. Or, with a *lot* of patience, you could reach the Wieskirche and Oberammergau by bus from Füssen—get details at the Füssen TI or at www.bahn.com.

Salzburg, Austria

Salzburg, just over the Austrian border, makes a fun day trip from Munich (1.5 hours by direct train). It has a charmingly preserved Old Town, a dramatic natural setting, Baroque churches, and one of Europe's largest medieval fortresses—Hohensalzburg. It's a musical mecca for fans of hometown-boy Mozart, the movie *The Sound of Music,* and classical-music concerts. Despite the tourist crowds, it's a city with class.

Salzburg is steeped in history. For a thousand years, it was an independent city (belonging to no state), ruled by a prince-bishop. These days, you can visit his hilltop fortress, his luxurious Residenz, or his fountain-spewing summer palace, Hellbrunn.

This chapter focuses on seeing Salzburg as a day trip from Munich. In a day, you could take my "Salzburg Old Town Walk," visit one, two, or

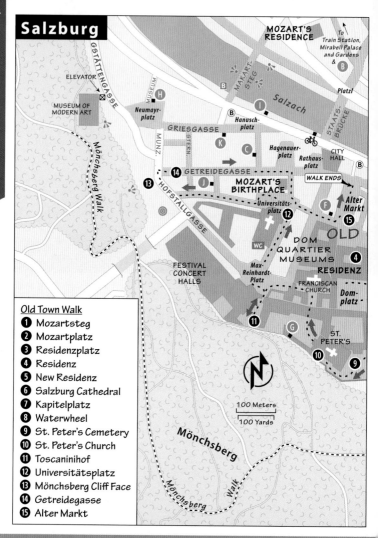

Salzburg

MOZART'S RESIDENCE

To Train Station, Mirabell Palace and Gardens &

Salzach

ELEVATOR

GSTÄTTENGASSE

MUSEUM OF MODERN ART

Mönchsberg Walk

MUSEUM

Neumayr-platz

H

Platzl

Hanusch-platz

GRIESGASSE

STERN

MÜNZ

K

C

Hagenauer-platz

Rathaus-platz

CITY HALL

STAATS-BRÜCKE

WALK ENDS

GETREIDEGASSE

MOZART'S BIRTHPLACE

Alter Markt

J

Universitäts-platz

F

OLD

WC

DOM QUARTIER MUSEUMS

RESIDENZ

FESTIVAL CONCERT HALLS

Max-Reinhardt-Platz

FRANCISCAN CHURCH

Dom-platz

ST. PETER'S

Mönchsberg

Mönchsberg Walk

100 Meters

100 Yards

Old Town Walk

1. Mozartsteg
2. Mozartplatz
3. Residenzplatz
4. Residenz
5. New Residenz
6. Salzburg Cathedral
7. Kapitelplatz
8. Waterwheel
9. St. Peter's Cemetery
10. St. Peter's Church
11. Toscaninihof
12. Universitätsplatz
13. Mönchsberg Cliff Face
14. Getreidegasse
15. Alter Markt

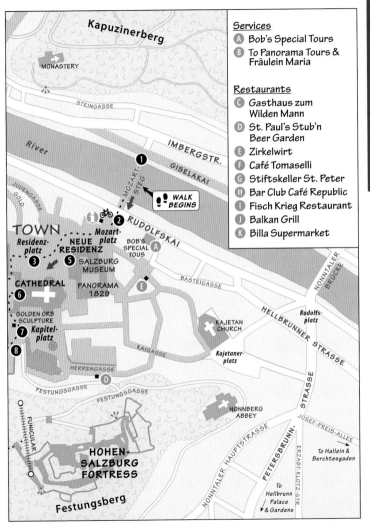

Services
- **A** Bob's Special Tours
- **B** To Panorama Tours & Fräulein Maria

Restaurants
- **C** Gasthaus zum Wilden Mann
- **D** St. Paul's Stub'n Beer Garden
- **E** Zirkelwirt
- **F** Café Tomaselli
- **G** Stiftskeller St. Peter
- **H** Bar Club Café Republic
- **I** Fisch Krieg Restaurant
- **J** Balkan Grill
- **K** Billa Supermarket

three other sights, and be back in Munich for a late-night beer. Salzburg also makes a great overnight stay, so I've recommended some hotels and restaurants, plus additional sights for those with more time.

Orientation to Salzburg

Getting There: Trains from Munich to Salzburg (and vice versa) run about twice per hour from early morning until nearly midnight. It costs about €65 round-trip, and takes 1.5 hours (2 hours on slower trains). The economical Regional Day Ticket for Bavaria works for Salzburg (see page 117). In fact, all rail passes that include Germany also include Salzburg (which is considered a border town). Salzburg's train station has a TI, luggage lockers, and a handy Spar supermarket.

Getting to the Old Town: From the train station, it's a snap. Simply step outside the train station, find **bus** platform C (labeled *Zentrum-Altstadt*), buy a ticket from the machine (€1.70 single-ride ticket, €3.40 day pass—*24-Stunden-Karte*), and hop on bus #1, #3, #5, #6, or #25. Get off just after you cross the river, at the fifth stop—either Rathaus or Hanuschplatz, depending on the bus. (To return to the train station, catch bus #1 from the inland side of Hanuschplatz.) A **taxi** into town (€2.50 drop charge) costs about €8.

Welcome to Austria: Austria uses the same euro currency as Germany, but postage stamps and phone cards only work in the country where you buy them. To make a telephone call in Austria, follow the same dialing instructions as for Germany (see page 171).

Tourist Information: There are helpful TIs at the train station (daily 9:00-18:00, tel. 0662/8898-7340) and on Mozartplatz in the old center (daily 9:00-18:00, closed Sun Sept-March, tel. 0662/8898-7330). The Mozartplatz TI has a box office for concert tickets. Get general tourist information at tel. 0662/889-870 or www.salzburg.info.

Salzburg Card: The TIs sell the Salzburg Card, which covers admission to all the city sights plus public transportation. The card is pricey (€24 for the 24-hour version), but even a day-tripper might make it pay for itself. Among its included sights are the Hohensalzburg Fortress with funicular ride (€11.30), Mozart's Birthplace (€10), DomQuartier Museums (€12), and Salzach River cruises (€15). For details see www.salzburg.info.

Walking Tours: Good-quality, one-hour guided group tours of the main sights leave daily at 12:15 and also at 14:00 (Mon-Sat). Just show up at the TI on Mozartplatz and pay the guide (€9, tel. 0662/8898-7330). For a private guide, I recommend Christiana Schneeweiss (€135/2 hours, can split cost up to six people, also offers minibus tours of the countryside, mobile 0664-340-1757, www.kultur-tourismus.com).

SALZBURG OLD TOWN WALK

Salzburg, a city of 150,000 (Austria's fourth-largest), is split in two by the Salzach River. North of the river lies the New Town (Neustadt), with the train station and a few sights.

But our walk focuses on the Old Town (Altstadt). Nestled between the Salzach River and Salzburg's mini-mountain (Mönchsberg), this neighborhood holds nearly all the charm and most of the tourists. (You can download a free Rick Steves audio tour of this walk; see page 173.)

▶ *Begin at the Mozartsteg, the pedestrian bridge over the Salzach River.*

❶ Mozartsteg

Take in the charming, well-preserved, historic core of Salzburg's Old Town. The skyline bristles with Baroque steeples and green, copper domes. Salzburg has 38 Catholic churches, plus two Protestant churches and a synagogue. The biggest green dome is the cathedral, which we'll visit shortly. Overlooking it all is the castle called the Hohensalzburg Fortress.

The milky-green Salzach River thunders under your feet. It's called "salt river" not because it's salty, but because of the precious cargo it once carried. The salt mines of Hallein are just nine miles upstream. For 2,000 years, barges carried the precious salt from here to the wider world. As

Start your Salzburg walk at the river.

Mozart statue on Mozartplatz by the TI

barges passed through, they had to pay a toll. So, the city was born from the trading of salt *(salz)* defended by a castle *(burg)*—"Salz-burg."

▶ *From the bridge, walk one block toward the hill-capping castle into the Old Town. Pass the traffic barriers and turn right into a big square—Mozartplatz.*

❷ Mozartplatz

The statue honors Wolfgang Amadeus Mozart. The great composer was born in Salzburg and spent most of his first 25 years (1756-1781) here. He and his father both served Salzburg's rulers before Wolfgang went on to seek his fortune in Vienna. The statue (considered a poor likeness) was erected in 1842 for the first small music festival that would eventually grow into the now world-renowned Salzburg Festival.

Mozart stands atop the spot where the first Salzburgers settled—the Roman salt-trading town called Juvavum. In the year 800, Salzburg—by then Christian and home to an important abbey—joined Charlemagne's Holy Roman Empire as an independent city. The Church of St. Michael (whose tower overlooks the square) dates from that time.

▶ *Note the TI, then walk toward the cathedral and into the big square with the huge fountain.*

❸ Residenzplatz

As Salzburg's governing center, this square has long been ringed with important buildings. The cathedral borders the south side. The Residenz—the former palace of Salzburg's rulers—is to the right (as you face the cathedral). To the left is the New Residenz, with its bell tower.

In the 1600s, this square got a makeover in the Italian Baroque style, under energetic Prince-Archbishop Wolf Dietrich (1559-1617). Dietrich had been raised in Rome, counted the Medicis as his cousins, and had grandiose Italian ambitions for Salzburg. When the cathedral conveniently burned down in 1598, Dietrich made it the centerpiece of his grand vision to make Salzburg the "Rome of the North."

The fountain is as Italian as can be, an over-the-top version of Bernini's famous Triton Fountain in Rome. It shows Triton on top blowing his conchshell horn. The water cascades down the basins and sprays playfully in the wind.

Notice that Salzburg's buildings are made from three distinctly different types of stone. Most common is the chunky gray conglomerate

An Italian Baroque fountain by the Baroque towers of the Cathedral—"The Rome of the North."

(like the cathedral's side walls), quarried from the nearby cliffs. There's also white marble (like the cathedral's towers and windows) and red marble (best seen in monuments inside buildings), both from the Alps near Berchtesgaden.

▶ *Turn your attention to the...*

❹ Residenz

This was the palace of Salzburg's powerful ruler, the prince-archbishop—that is, a ruler with both the political powers of a prince and the religious authority of an archbishop. For centuries, the prince-archbishops ruled Salzburg as their own little kingdom—a city-state that was not a part of any larger nation. The ornate Baroque entrance attests to the connections these rulers had with Rome. You can step inside the Residenz courtyard to get a glimpse of the impressive digs. To see the Residenz' fancy interior you must buy a DomQuartier ticket (for details, see page 148).

▶ *At the opposite end of Residenzplatz from the Residenz is the...*

❺ New (Neue) Residenz

The prince-archbishops hosted parties in the New Residenz' lavish rooms. These days, it houses the Salzburg Museum and Salzburg Panorama 1829 (see page 149), as well as a fine shop of local handicrafts.

The New Residenz bell tower has a famous glockenspiel. This 17th-century carillon has 35 bells (cast in Antwerp) and chimes daily at 7:00, 11:00, and 18:00.

▶ *Exit the square by walking under the prince-archbishop's skyway—so he could commute to work high above the unwashed masses. You'll step into Cathedral Square (Domplatz). A good place to view the cathedral facade is from the far end of the square.*

❻ Salzburg Cathedral (Salzburger Dom)

The cathedral (1628) was the first Baroque church north of the Alps. The dome stands 230 feet high. Two domed towers flank the entrance. Between them is a false-front roofline. The windows are flanked with classical half-columns and topped with heavy pediments. The facade is ringed with a Baroque balustrade, decorated with garlands and masks, and studded with statues. It dates from the years of Catholic-Protestant warfare, and its Italian style emphasized that Salzburg was the northern outpost of the Catholic Church—the "Rome of the North."

In the square, the **statue of Mary** (1771) is looking away from the church, welcoming visitors. Photo tip: If you view the statue from the rear of the square (immediately under the middle arch), she appears to be crowned Queen of Heaven by the two angels on the church facade.

Now, approach the church. The iron entrance doors have dates marking milestones in the church's history: In the year 774, the first church was consecrated by St. Virgil (see his statue), an Irish monk who became Salzburg's bishop. In 1598, the church burned. In 1628, it was replaced by the church you see today. In 1959, the church was renovated after being severely damaged by a bomb in World War II.

▶ *More about that inside.*

The statue of Mary in front of Salzburg Cathedral being "crowned" by angels on the facade

Cathedral Interior

The cathedral is free to enter (May-Sept Mon-Sat 9:00-19:00, Sun 13:00-19:00; closes earlier off-season; www.salzburger-dom.at). The interior is clean and white, without excess decoration. Because it was built in just 14 years (from 1614 to 1628), the church boasts harmonious architecture. And it's big—330 feet long, 230 feet tall—built with sturdy pillars and broad arches. When Pope John Paul II visited in 1998, some 5,000 people packed the place.

At the back pew, black-and-white photos show the bomb damage of October 16,1944, which left a gaping hole where the dome once was. In the first chapel on the left is a dark bronze baptismal font. It dates from 1320—a rare survivor from the medieval cathedral. In 1756, little Wolfgang Amadeus Mozart was baptized here. For the next 25 years, this would be his home church.

Now make your way up the nave, drawn to the light of the altar area. Under the soaring dome, look up and admire the exceptional (Italian-style) stucco work. It's molded into elaborate garlands, angels, and picture frames, some of it brightly painted. You're surrounded by the tombs (and portraits) of 10 archbishops.

You're also surrounded by four organs. (Actually, five, counting the biggest organ, over the entrance.) Mozart served as organist here for two years, and he composed several Masses still played today. Salzburg's prince-archbishops were great patrons of music, with a personal orchestra that played religious music in the cathedral and dinner music in the Residenz. The tradition of music continues today. Sunday Mass here can be a musical spectacle—all five organs playing, balconies filled with singers and musicians, creating glorious surround-sound. Think of the altar in

The Cathedral Mass has world-class music.

Modern art in this cultured city

Baroque terms, as the center of a stage, with sunrays serving as spotlights in this dramatic and sacred theater.

▶ *As you leave the cathedral, turn left. You'll soon enter a spacious square with a golden orb.*

❼ Kapitelplatz

The playful modern sculpture in the square (from 2007) shows a man atop a golden orb, gazing up the hill to **Hohensalzburg Fortress.** (I think he's trying to decide whether to take the funicular up or save a few euros by hiking up.) Construction of the fortress began in 1077. Over the centuries, the small castle grew into a mighty, whitewashed fortress—so impressive that no army even tried attacking for over 800 years. These days, you can tour it (see page 150). Today's electric-powered **funicular** is from 1910, but the rails actually date from as far back as the 1500s, when animals pulled cargo up to the fortress. (Take note of *Festungsgasse,* the street that exits Kapitelplatz and leads up to the fortress and the funicular station.)

Continue across the square to the balustraded pond adorned with a Trevi-Fountain-like statue of Neptune. It looks fancy, but the pond was built as a horse bath, the 18th-century equivalent of a car wash. Notice the gold lettering above Neptune. It reads, "Leopold the Prince Built Me." But the artist added a clever twist. The inscription uses the letters "LLDVI," and so on. Those are also Roman numerals—add 'em up: L is 50, D is 500, and so on. It all adds up to 1732—the year the pond was built.

▶ *Now, with your back to the cathedral, leave the square, exiting through the right corner. You'll pass by a sign on a building that reads* zum Peterskeller—*to St. Peter's Cemetery. But first, you reach a waterwheel.*

❽ Waterwheel

The waterwheel—overlooked by a statue of St. Peter—is part of a clever 13th-century canal system that still brings water to Salzburg from the foothills of the Alps, 10 miles away. The rushing water was harnessed to waterwheels, which powered factories. This particular waterwheel (actually, it's a modern replacement) once ground grain into flour to make bread for the monks of St. Peter's Abbey. Nowadays, you can pop into the adjacent bakery—fragrant and traditional—and buy a fresh-baked roll for about a euro.

▶ *You've entered the borders of the former St. Peter's Abbey, a monastic complex of churches, courtyards, businesses (like the bakery), and a*

Waterwheel of the former Abbey

Graves and churches of St. Peter's Cemetery

cemetery. Find the Katakomben *sign and step through the wrought-iron gates into...*

9 St. Peter's Cemetery

This collection of lovingly tended graves abuts the sheer rock face of the Mönchsberg (free, silence requested; open daily June-Aug 6:30-21:30, April-May until 20:00, closes earlier off-season, www.stift-stpeter.at). Walk in about 30 yards to the middle of the cemetery. You're surrounded by three churches, each founded in the early Middle Ages atop a pagan Celtic holy site. The biggest church, St. Peter's, sticks its big Romanesque apse into the cemetery.

The graves surrounding you are tended by descendants of the deceased. In Austria (and many other European countries), gravesites are rented, not owned. If no one cares enough to make the payment, your tombstone is removed.

The cemetery plays a role in *The Sound of Music*. In the movie, this was where the von Trapp family hid behind tombstones from the Nazis. (The scene was actually filmed on a Hollywood set, inspired by St. Peter's Cemetery.)

Look up the cliff, which has a few buildings attached—called **"catacombs"**—where legendary medieval hermit monks are said to have lived. You can visit these caves—the *Katakomben* entrance is at the base of the cliff, under the arcade (€2, visit takes 10 minutes; daily May-Sept 10:00-12:00 & 13:00-18:00, Oct-April until 17:00).

Explore the arcade at the base of the cliff with its various burial chapels. Alcove #XXI has the tomb of the cathedral architect—forever facing his creation. #LIV has two interesting tombs marked by plaques on the floor. "Marianne" is Mozart's sister, nicknamed Nannerl. Michael Haydn was the brother of Joseph Haydn. He succeeded Mozart as church cathedral organist.

▶ *Exit the cemetery at the opposite end. Just outside, you enter a large courtyard anchored by...*

⑩ St. Peter's Church (Stiftskirche St. Peter)

You're standing at the birthplace of Christianity in Salzburg. St. Peter's Abbey—the monastery that surrounds this courtyard—was founded in 696, barely two centuries after the fall of Rome. The recommended Stiftskeller St. Peter restaurant in the courtyard brags that Charlemagne ate here in the year 803, making it (perhaps) the oldest restaurant in Europe.

St. Peter's Church dates from 1147 (free, daily April-Oct 8:00-21:00, Nov-March until 19:00, www.stift-stpeter.at). Entering the church, pause in the atrium to admire the Romanesque tympanum (from 1250) over the inner doorway. Jesus sits on a rainbow, flanked by Peter and Paul, with a Latin inscription reading, "I am the door to life."

Christ presides over the church entrance at St. Peter's Abbey, where Christian Salzburg began.

Inside, you'll find Salzburg's only Rococo interior—all whitewashed, with highlights of pastel green, gold, and red. The ceiling paintings feature St. Peter receiving the keys from Christ (center painting), walking on water, and joining the angels in heaven.

The monastery was founded by St. Rupert (c. 650-718). Find his statue at the main altar—he's the second gold statue from the left. Rupert arrived as a Christian missionary, converted the pagans, reopened the Roman salt mines, and established the city, naming it "Salzburg." Rupert's tomb is midway up the right aisle.

▶ *Exit the courtyard at the opposite side from where you entered. The passageway leads to a T-intersection (where you bump into the Franzis-kanerkirche). Turn left. Pass beneath an archway, and enter a square (Max-Reinhardt-Platz). Pause to admire the line of impressive Salzburg Festival concert halls ahead of you. Then turn left, through an arch, into a small square called...*

⑪ Toscaninihof

In this small courtyard, you get a peek at the back end of the large Festival Hall complex. The Festival Hall, built in 1925, has three theaters and seats 5,000 people. It's very busy during the Salzburg Music Festival each summer. When the festival was started in the 1920s, they transformed a former horse stables into this concert hall.

The tunnel you see (behind the *Felsenkeller* sign) leads to the actual concert hall. It's generally closed, but occasionally, you can look through nearby doorways and see carpenters building stage sets for an upcoming show.

The von Trapp family performed in the Festival Hall. In the movie, this courtyard is where Captain von Trapp nervously waited before walking onstage to sing "Edelweiss."

▶ *Return to Max-Reinhardt-Platz. Continue straight, heading downhill, along the right side of the big church. As you stroll, you'll pass by popular sausage stands, offering the best of the wurst. You'll pass by a public toilet, and enter Universitätsplatz.*

⑫ Universitätsplatz

This square hosts Salzburg's liveliest open-air produce market (generally open Mon-Sat mornings). It's best early on Saturday, when the farmers are in town.

The fancy yellow facade overlooking the square marks the back end of Mozart's Birthplace, which we'll see shortly. Find the fountain—it's about 30 yards along. As with public marketplaces elsewhere, it's for washing fruit and vegetables. The sundial over the drain hole shows both the time (easy to decipher) and the date (less obvious).

▶ *Continue toward the end of the square. Along the way, you'll pass several nicely arcaded medieval passageways (on the right), which lead to Salzburg's old main street, Getreidegasse.*

⑬ Mönchsberg Cliff Face

Rising 200 feet above you is the Mönchsberg, Salzburg's mountain. This served as a quarry for the city's 17th-century growth spurt—the bulk of the cathedral, for example, is built of this conglomerate stone. At the base of the cliff are giant horse troughs, for the prince-archbishops' prized horses. Paintings show the various breeds. Like Vienna, Salzburg had a passion for the equestrian arts.

▶ *Before turning right onto Getreidegasse, take note of the elevator up to the Mönchsberg just ahead, which leads to a pleasant walk along the ridgeline (see the "Mönchsberg Walk" on page 151). Now retrace your steps and turn left onto Getreidegasse.*

⑭ Getreidegasse

Old Salzburg's colorful main drag, Getreidegasse has been a center of trade since Roman times. The buildings date mainly from the 15th century. These days the street bustles with the tourist trade. Check out all the old wrought-iron signs that—then as now—advertise what's sold inside. There are signs advertising spirits, a bookmaker, and a horn indicating a place

Upscale horse trough by the Mönchsberg

Getreidegasse—each shop has an ID sign

for the postal coach. There's a window maker, a key maker, a tailor, a pretzel maker, a pharmacy, a hat maker, and...ye olde hamburger shoppe, McDonald's.

Sample homemade spirits at Sporer (#39) or ice cream at Eisgrotte (#40). At #28 (a blacksmith shop since the 1400s), Herr Wieber welcomes the curious. At Getreidegasse #9, the knot of excited tourists marks the birthplace of Salzburg's most famous resident—Mozart (see page 149).

▸ *At Getreidegasse #3, turn right, into the passageway. When you reach the venerable Schatz Konditorei (worth a stop for a pastry), turn left, through the passage. When you reach Sigmund-Haffner-Gasse, glance to the left (for a nice view of the city hall tower), then turn right. Walk along Sigmund-Haffner-Gasse and take your first left, to reach a square called...*

⑮ Alter Markt

This is Salzburg's old marketplace. Here you'll find a sausage stand, the esteemed Café Tomaselli, and a fun candy shop at #7. Next door is the beautifully old-fashioned Alte F. E. Hofapotheke pharmacy—duck in discreetly (no photos) to peek at the Baroque shelves and containers.

▸ *Our walk is over. If you're up for more sightseeing, you're right in the center of it all. Read on.*

MORE SIGHTS IN SALZBURG

The best Old Town sights are linked in my self-guided walk, earlier. I've covered some of those sights in more detail below. I've also listed a few other sightseeing options if you have extra time.

In the Old Town

▲DomQuartier Museums

The DomQuartier ticket admits you to the world of the prince-archbishops. You visit several historic buildings and small museums in the Residenz/Cathedral part of town.

In the Residenz State Rooms—once the prince-archbishop's palace—you walk through 15 chandeliered, stuccoed, and frescoed rooms. In the painting collection, Rubens' *The Allegory on Charles V* shows the pope's great champion with a sword in one hand and a scepter in the other. Rembrandt's teeny-tiny *Old Woman Praying/Rembrandt's Mother* glows, despite her wrinkled face and broken teeth. Next, you visit the Cathedral (which you view from the organ loft) and several small museums on religious art. Your final stop is the Museum of St. Peter's Abbey, introducing you to work and life at the abbey.

▶ €12, Wed-Mon 10:00-17:00, closed Tue except in July-Aug, last tickets sold at 16:00, includes audioguide, Residenzplatz 1, tel. 0662/8042-2109, www.domquartier.at.

▲▲Salzburg Museum and Salzburg Panorama 1829

This is your best look at Salzburg's history, displayed in lavish rooms where Salzburg's rulers entertained. The permanent exhibit called The Salzburg Myth tells how the town's physical beauty and music festival attracted 19th-century Romantic nobles, making it Europe's first tourist destination. Next comes the glory days of the prince-archbishops (1500-1800), with their portraits displayed in impressive ceremonial rooms. Room 2.11—a big, colorful hall—showcases the most famous prince-archbishop, Wolf Dietrich von Raitenau, the Renaissance Man who largely created the city we see today.

In an adjoining building is the ▲ **Salzburg Panorama 1829,** a painting that surrounds you with a 360-degree view of the city in 1829.

▶ Salzburg Museum—€7, €8.50 combo-ticket with Salzburg Panorama 1829; open Tue-Sun 9:00-17:00, closed Mon; includes so-so audioguide, tel. 0662/620-8080, www.salzburgmuseum.at. Salzburg Panorama—€3, open daily 9:00-17:00, Residenzplatz 9, tel. 0662/620-808-730.

▲▲Mozart's Birthplace (Geburtshaus)

In 1747, Leopold Mozart—a musician in the prince-archbishop's band—moved into this small rental unit with his new bride. Soon they had a baby girl (Nannerl) and, in 1756, a little boy was born—Wolfgang Amadeus Mozart. It was here that Mozart learned to play piano and violin and composed his first boy-genius works. Even after the family gained fame, touring Europe's palaces and becoming the toast of Salzburg, they continued living in this rather cramped apartment.

Today, you'll peruse three floors of exhibits: portraits of the famous family, Mozart's small-size childhood violin, some (possible) locks of his

Mozart's Salzburg

Salzburg was Mozart's home for the first 25 years of his brief, 35-year life. He was born on Getreidegasse and baptized in the cathedral. He played his first big concert, at age six, at the Residenz. He was the organist for the Cathedral, conducted the prince-archbishop's orchestra, and dined at (what's now called) Café Tomaselli. It was from Salzburg that he gained Europe-wide fame, touring the continent with his talented performing family. At age 17, Mozart and his family moved into lavish digs at (today's) Mozart's Residence.

As his fame and ambitions grew, Mozart eventually left Salzburg to pursue his dreams in Vienna. His departure from Salzburg's royal court in 1781 is the stuff of legend. Mozart, full of himself, announced that he was quitting. The prince-archbishop essentially said, "You can't quit; you're fired!" and as Mozart walked out, he was literally kicked in the ass.

hair, buttons from his jacket, and a letter to his wife, whom he calls his "little rascal, pussy-pussy."

The museum also chronicles Mozart's life after he left Salzburg and moved to Vienna, achieved even greater fame (especially with operas), then fell on hard times and died young and poor. The finale is an old clavichord on which Mozart supposedly composed his final work—the *Requiem,* which was played for his own funeral.

▸ *€10, €17 combo-ticket with Mozart's Residence, daily July-Aug 8:30-19:00, Sept-June 9:00-17:30, Getreidegasse 9, tel. 0662/844-313, www.mozarteum.at. Avoid the shoulder-to-shoulder crowds by visiting right when it opens or late in the day.*

Atop the Cliffs, Above the New Town

▲▲Hohensalzburg Fortress (Festung)

Built on a rock 400 feet above the Salzach River, this mighty castle has overlooked the Old Town for a thousand years. Today, it offers incredible views, pleasant cafés, and a handful of mediocre museums about medieval history.

Mozart's presence permeates his hometown.

A pleasant courtyard at Hohensalzburg Fort

You can walk there—it's a steep but paved walk from Kapitelplatz (next to the cathedral) up Festungsgasse. Or (for €3.30 more) take the funicular *(Festungsbahn)* that starts from the foot of Festungsgasse.

The fortress is an eight-acre complex of some 50 buildings, courtyards, and protective walls. The exhibit called **Tour A** features a few (mostly bare) castle rooms, medieval torture implements, and a commanding view from the top of a tower. As you exit, pause at the "Salzburger Bull," a mechanical barrel organ used to wake the citizens every morning. The **Tour B—The Fortress Museum (Festungsmuseum)** exhibit shows how the fortress was constructed, along with everyday medieval objects (dishes, ovens), weapons (pikes, cannons), old musical instruments, more torture devices (including a chastity belt), and some large ceremonial rooms. The recently restored **Regency Rooms (Tour C),** are the most beautiful in the palace.

The **Marionette Exhibit** has puppets and scenery backdrops of this Salzburg tradition (think "Lonely Goatherd" scene in *The Sound of Music*). Give the hands-on marionette a whirl, and find Wolf Dietrich in a Box.

▶ *€8.20-11.50, €12-15.20 with round-trip funicular, various tickets cover different parts of fortress. Museums open daily year-round (May-Sept 9:00-19:00, Oct-April 9:30-17:00). The grounds stay open after hours and the funicular continues to run (€4 round-trip) until about 22:00. The Salzburg Card lets you skip to the head of the line for the often-crowded funicular. To avoid crowds (especially in summer), visit early in the morning or late in the day. Tel. 0662/8424-3011, www.salzburg-burgen.at.*

▲Mönchsberg Walk

The bluff overlooking the city has a paved walking path stretching a mile between the Hohensalzburg Fortress and the Mönchsberg elevator. It's mostly level, well-signed, and easy to do. The views of Salzburg are the main draw, but there's also a modern art museum, mansions to ogle, and a couple of places for a scenic drink. You can start from either end: at the Fortress or at the Mönchsberg elevator (at Gstättengasse 13, €2.10 one-way, normally Tue-Sun 8:00-23:00, Mon 8:00-19:00).

In the New Town, North of the River

▲Mozart's Residence (Wohnhaus)

In the fall of 1773, when Wolfgang was 17—and his family was flush with money from years of touring—the Mozarts moved here from their cramped apartment on Getreidegasse. The exhibits here are aimed a bit more toward the Mozart connoisseur than those at Mozart's Birthplace, and it's less crowded, but either place will fill the bill—no need to do both.

In the main hall—where the Mozarts entertained Salzburg's high society—you'll see Wolfgang's very own piano, his violin, and a family portrait. Other exhibits highlight Wolfgang's father Leopold (a loving nurturer of young Mozart or an exploiting Svengali?) and Mozart's sister Nannerl (Wolfgang's fellow child prodigy who grew up to lead a stable life as wife and mother). By the time Mozart was 25, he'd grown tired of his father, this house, and Salzburg, and he went on to Vienna—to more triumphs, but ultimately, a sad end.

▶ *€10, €17 combo-ticket with Mozart's Birthplace, daily July-Aug 8:30-19:00, Sept-June 9:00-17:30, Makartplatz 8, tel. 0662/8742-2740, www.mozarteum.at.*

Beyond the Center

▲▲Hellbrunn Palace and Gardens

The prince-archbishops' summer palace—four miles outside the city—is a nice getaway. Upon arrival, you sign up for the next departing **fountain tour.** The 40-minute tours take you laughing through an amazing 17th-century garden where you get soaked by trick fountains. Then you're free to wander the delightful garden, see the *Sound of Music* gazebo, and tour the modest palace.

▶ *€10.50, daily May-Sept 9:00-17:30, July-Aug until 21:00, April and Oct 9:00-16:30, closed Nov-March, tel. 0662/820-3720, www.hellbrunn.at.*

Trick fountain at Hellbrunn Palace

Salzburg by bike—with a group or alone

Getting There: *Take bus #25 from the train station or the Rathaus stop by the Staatsbrücke bridge (2-3/hour, 20 minutes). With a rental bike, it's a pleasant 30-minute excursion (see "Bike Rides" under "Activities in Salzburg").*

Sights Outside Salzburg

If you have more time, you can day-trip to the nearby **Hallein Salt Mine** (www.salzwelten.at) or **Berchtesgaden** (alpine scenery and Hitler's Eagle's Nest retreat, www.berchtesgadener-land.info).

ACTIVITIES IN SALZBURG

▲▲*The Sound of Music* Tours

Salzburg is the joyful setting of *The Sound of Music.* The 1965 movie tells the story of a stern captain who hires a governess for his unruly children and ends up marrying her. Though the movie took plenty of Hollywood liberties, it's based on the actual von Trapp family from Austria. They really did come from Salzburg. Maria really was a governess who became the captain's wife. They did sing in the Festival Hall, they did escape from the Nazis, and they ended up after the war in Vermont, where Maria passed away in 1987.

Salzburg today has a number of *Sound of Music* sights—mostly locations where the movie was shot, but also some actual places associated with the von Trapps. Since they're scattered throughout greater Salzburg, taking a tour is the best way to see them efficiently. An added bonus is it gets you outside the city center into some lovely countryside.

By Minibus: For a casual, fun approach to the *Sound of Music* (that may even include a luge ride), **Bob's Special Tours** hits all the sights in a four-hour tour. You must reserve in advance—online (at least 3 days in advance) or by email, phone, or in person (€48, daily at 9:00 and 14:00 year-round, Rudolfskai 38, tel. 0662/849-511, mobile 0664-541-7492, www.bobstours.com). For a private minibus tour, consider **Christina Schneeweiss** (€240, split cost up to 6 people, mobile 0664-340-1757, www.kultur-tourismus.com).

By Big Tour Bus: Panorama Tours is more businesslike, with roomier buses and a high vantage point (€40, daily at 9:15 and 14:00 year-round, reserve at 0662/874-029 or www.panoramatours.com).

By Bike: For some fun exercise with your *S.O.M.* tour, the **"Fräulein Maria"** company offers eight-mile, 3.5-hour bike tours (€26 includes bike, daily May-Sept at 9:30, June-Aug also at 16:30, Mirabellplatz 4, reserve at mobile 0650-342-6297, www.mariasbicycletours.com).

Bike Rides

Salzburg is great fun for cyclists. A simple ride along the Salzach River—with flat bike lanes on either side—is scenic and easy.

Or take a four-mile path to Hellbrunn Palace. Head east along the river on Rudolfskai. After passing the last bridge (Nonntaler Brücke), cut inland along Petersbrunnstrasse, until you reach the university and Akademiestrasse. Beyond it find the start of Freisaalweg, which becomes the delightful Hellbrunner Allee bike path...which leads directly to the palace.

Top Bike rents bikes next to the Staatsbrücke bridge (€6/2 hours, daily April-Oct 10:00-17:00, may be open longer hours, closed Nov-March, mobile 0676-476-7259, www.topbike.at). **A'Velo Radladen** rents bikes by the TI on Mozartplatz (€4.50/1 hour, usually daily 9:00-18:00, shorter hours off-season and in bad weather, mobile 0676-435-5950, www.a-velo.at). Some hotels also loan bikes to guests.

Buggy Rides

The horse buggies *(Fiaker)* that congregate at Residenzplatz charge €40 for a 25-minute trot around the Old Town (www.fiaker-salzburg.at).

Boat Cruises on the Salzach

City Cruise Line (a.k.a. Stadt Schiff-Fahrt) boats depart almost hourly from

- The Mirabell Gardens, with its arbor and Pegasus statue, where the kids sing "Do-Re-Mi."
- Festival Hall, where the real-life von Trapps performed, and where (in the movie) they sing "Edelweiss."

- St. Peter's Cemetery, the inspiration for the scene where the family hides from Nazi guards (it was actually filmed on a Hollywood set).
- Nonnberg Abbey, where the nuns sing "How Do You Solve a Problem like Maria?"
- Leopoldskron Palace, which serves as the von Trapps' idyllic lakeside home in the movie (though it wasn't their actual home).
- Hellbrunn Palace gardens, where the famous gazebo in "I am Sixteen" has found a home.
- Along the Old Town Walk, you'll see quick scene-setting shots of the fountain in Residenzplatz and the horse pond.

Makartsteg bridge for a basic 40-minute round-trip river cruise with recorded commentary (€15, no boats Nov-Feb, tel. 0662/825-858, www.salzburghighlights.at).

MUSIC IN SALZBURG

Almost any night of the year, you'll find classical music concerts held in historic settings. Pick up the free events calendar at the TI or check www.salzburg.info (under "Art & Culture," click on "Music"). Here are some of the perennial venues:

Classical Concerts: Hohensalzburg Fortress (Festungskonzerte) has chamber ensembles playing Mozart's greatest hits in a medieval

Enjoy classical music at classy venues.

Tasty chocolate "Mozart balls"

hall (€40, reserve at tel. 0662/825-858 or www.salzburghighlights. at). **Mirabell Palace (Schlosskonzerte)** offers more sophisticated programs, in a Baroque setting (€35, ask about Rick discount, tel. 0662/828-695, www.salzburg-palace-concerts.com). With the **Mozart Dinner Concert,** you get a candlelit dinner in the historic Stiftskeller restaurant (see next section) along with your Mozart music (€56, dress is "smart casual," reserve by phone or email, tel. 0662/828-695, www. mozart-dinner-concert-salzburg.com, office@skg.co.at).

Sunday Morning Mass at Salzburg Cathedral: The 10:00 service generally features a Mass written by a well-known composer performed by choir, organist, or other musicians. The worship service is often followed at 11:30 by a free organ concert (music program at www.kirchen. net/dommusik).

Marionette Theater: These operettas with puppets, a much-loved Salzburg tradition, enchant kids and adults (€25, Schwarzstrasse 24, tel. 0662/872-406, www.marionetten.at).

Salzburg Music Festival: The famous music festival in July and August brings large crowds. Hotels fill up. Major musical events are expensive (€50-600) and sell out well in advance (bookable from January, www. salzburgfestival.at).

SLEEPING AND EATING IN SALZBURG

Sleeping

These two hotels are centrally located in the Old Town, near Mozartplatz. **$$$ Hotel am Dom** (tel. 0662/842-765, Goldgasse 17, www.hotelamdom.at). **$$$ Hotel Weisse Taube** (Kaigasse 9, tel. 0662/842-404, www.weissetaube.at).

These three places are in the New Town (north of the river), near a lively pedestrian street, a 10-minute walk from the Old Town. **$$$ Altstadthotel Wolf-Dietrich** (Wolf-Dietrich-Strasse 7, tel. 0662/871-275, www.salzburg-hotel.at). **$$ Hotel Trumer Stube** (Bergstrasse 6, tel. 0662/874-776, www.trumer-stube.at). **$ International Youth Hostel** (mainly dorm beds but some doubles, Paracelsusstrasse 9, tel. 0662/879-649, www.yoho.at).

Outside of downtown, these good-value, rural, family-run pensions are an easy 15-minute ride from the Old Town on handy bus #21. **$$ Pension Bloberger Hof** (Hammerauer Strasse 4, tel. 0662/830-227, www.blobergerhof.at). **$ Haus Ballwein** (Moosstrasse 69a, tel. 0662/824-029, www.haus-ballwein.at).

Eating

The following places are conveniently located in the Old Town. In Austria, restaurants must either be smoke-free (marked with a green sticker on the door) or allow smoking with some smoke-free zones (red stickers). For locations, see the map on page 134.

$ Gasthaus zum Wilden Mann serves hearty peasant fare at friendly shared tables in a well-antlered room (Mon-Sat 11:00-21:00, closed Sun, enter from Getreidegasse 22, tel. 0662/841-787, www.wildermann.co.at). **$$ St. Paul's Stub'n Beer Garden** is bohemian-chic with above-average beer-hall fare in troll-like rooms or tree-shaded garden, reservations smart (Mon-Sat 17:00-22:00, closed Sun, Herrengasse 16, tel. 0662/843-220, http://paulstubm.blogspot.com). **Zirkelwirt** serves schnitzel, goulash, *Spätzle* with kraut, and big salads away from tourist crowds (daily 11:00-24:00, Pfeifergasse 14, tel. 0662/842-796, www.zumzirkelwirt.at).

$ Café Tomaselli has pastries, drinks, and light meals in an elegant (but unstuffy) setting (daily 7:00-20:00, Alter Markt 9, tel. 0662/844-488, www.tomaselli.at). **$$$ Stiftskeller St. Peter** is historic, classy, and high-end touristy, serving uninspired Austrian favorites (daily 11:30-22:00

or later, by St. Peter's Church—see page 145 of the "Salzburg Old Town Walk," tel. 0662/841-268, www.haslauer.at). **$$ Bar Club Café Republic** is hip, untouristy and un-wursty, with modern international fare and cocktails (daily 8:00-late, Anton-Neumayr-Platz 2, tel. 0662/841-613, www. republic-cafe.at).

For cheaper fare, **$ Fisch Krieg Restaurant,** on the river, serves great-value, fast, fresh fish in a self-service dining room or riverside terrace (Mon-Fri 8:30-18:30, Sat 8:30-13:00, closed Sun, Hanuschplatz 4, tel. 0662/843-732, www.fisch-krieg.at). **$ Balkan Grill,** a Salzburg institution, has great take-out wursts (Mon-Sat 11:00-19:00, Sun 15:00-19:00, enter at Getreidegasse 33). **$ Billa supermarket** is well-stocked for picnic shoppers (open daily, Griesgasse 19a).

Mellow Pub Crawl: Start at Staatsbrücke bridge and head east along **Steingasse.** You'll find an interesting bar about every hundred yards, catering to well-dressed locals lazily smoking cigarettes and talking philosophy to laid-back tunes.

Salzburg—the Old Town and Hohensalzburg Fortress (on the hill), bordered by the Salzach River

Practicalities

PLANNING

When to Go

Munich's best travel months—also the busiest and most expensive for flights and hotels—are roughly May through September. Summer brings the best weather (it's rarely too hot), long sightseeing days, and big tourist crowds. "Shoulder season" (late April and early Oct) is a bit less expensive and less crowded, with decent weather and more flexible hotel prices. Munich's whole atmosphere changes during Oktoberfest (late Sept-early Oct), when huge crowds converge here, hotel prices skyrocket, and you're either part of the party or annoyed by the inconvenience. Munich in winter is cold and rainy, but the crowds are less, beer halls are cozy, Christmas markets bustle, and the concert seasons are in full swing.

Before You Go

Make sure your passport is up to date (to renew, see www.travel.state. gov). Tell your debit- and credit-card companies about your plans. Book hotel rooms as soon as you know your schedule, especially April through June, September, October, and especially for Oktoberfest and other festivals (find a list at www.germany.travel). Consider buying travel insurance (see www.ricksteves.com/insurance). Munich's museums don't require long-range planning for advance tickets, but consider reserving ahead if you're visiting Neuschwanstein Castle, especially for July and August (see page 113). If you're traveling beyond Germany, train travelers should check into rail passes, and car rental is easiest from the States.

MONEY

Germany (and Austria) use the euro currency: 1 euro (€1) = about $1.20. To convert euros to dollars, add about 20 percent: €20 = about $24, €50 = about $60. (Check www.oanda.com for the latest exchange rates.)

Withdraw money from an ATM (known as a *Geldautomat* in Germany; *Bankomat* in Austria) using a debit card, just like at home. Visa and MasterCard are commonly used throughout Europe. Before departing, call your bank or credit-card company: Confirm that your card will work overseas, ask about international transaction fees, and alert them that you'll be making withdrawals in Europe. Many travelers bring a second debit/credit

Helpful Websites

Munich Tourist Information: www.muenchen.de
German Tourist Information: www.germany.travel
Passports and Red Tape: www.travel.state.gov
Cheap Flights: www.kayak.com
Airplane Carry-on Restrictions: www.tsa.gov
European Train Schedules: www.bahn.com
General Travel Tips: www.ricksteves.com (helpful info on train travel, railpasses, car rental, using your mobile device, travel insurance, packing lists, and much more—plus updates to this book)

card as a backup. Compared to the US, Germany is a cash-focused country. Be prepared to pay with cash, as many vendors won't take plastic or will charge you extra for the privilege. Withdraw large amounts (€250-300) from the ATM.

While American magnetic-stripe credit cards are accepted almost everywhere in Europe, they may not work in some automated payment machines (e.g., ticket kiosks) geared for European-style chip-and-pin cards. Be prepared to pay with cash, try entering your card's PIN, or find a nearby cashier.

To keep your cash and valuables safe, wear a money belt. But if you do lose your credit or debit card, report the loss immediately with a phone call: Visa (tel. 303/967-1096), MasterCard (tel. 636/722-7111), and American Express (tel. 336/393-1111).

ARRIVAL IN MUNICH

Munich Airport
Munich's airport has two terminals with a small shopping center in between (airport code: MUC, tel. 089/97500, www.munich-airport.de). Allow 10 minutes to walk between terminals or catch a shuttle bus. To get between the airport and downtown Munich (25 miles away), you have several options:

Subway: It's an easy 40-minute ride to Marienplatz or the train station on the S-1 or S-8, which run every 20 minutes (from 4:00 to almost 2:00 in the morning). A single ticket for this trip costs €10.40. Consider buying a pass instead: The €11.70 Munich *Gesamtnetz* day pass (a.k.a. the "Airport-City-Day-Ticket") covers public transportation all day and pays for itself with just one more journey. Groups of two or more should buy the €21.30 Munich *Gesamtnetz* partner day pass, which gives up to five adults the run of the system for the day.

To buy a ticket or pass at a ticket machine, first press "MVV Münchner Verkehrs-und Tarifverbund," which displays the array of ticket options. No need to validate a pass bought at a ticket machine. The trip is free with a validated and dated rail pass. The S-8 is a bit quicker and easier, as the S-1 line has two branches and some trains split. For the trip from downtown to the airport, if you take the S-1, be certain your train is going to the *Flughafen*. (For more on riding Munich's transit system, see page 166.)

Lufthansa Airport Bus: The €10.50 bus makes the 45-minute journey between the airport (both terminals) and the main train station. Buy tickets on the bus. To catch the bus from the train station, exit out the north side, near track 26, and look for yellow *Airport Bus* signs (3/hour, buses depart train station 5:15-19:55, www.airportbus-muenchen.de).

Taxi: It's a long, expensive drive. It's better to take public transport and then switch to a taxi if needed.

Munich's Main Train Station (Hauptbahnhof)

Munich's main train station (München Hauptbahnhof) sits on the west edge of the tourist center—a 15-minute walk to Marienplatz, a five-minute walk to many recommended hotels, or a short ride on public transit to almost anywhere in Munich. Many of the city's subways, trams, and buses stop here.

The station is a sight in itself—one of those places that can turn a homebody into a carefree vagabond. Near track 26, you'll find lockers, pay public toilets and showers (downstairs), and a Yorma's mini-mart (good sandwiches). The bright food court is by track 14.

You'll find a city-run TI (out front of station and to the right) and the EurAide desk (by track 21). The k presse + buch shop (track 23) has English-language books, newspapers, and magazines. Radius Tours (at track 32) rents bikes and organizes tours (see pages 168 and 116).

Up the stairs opposite track 21 are car-rental agencies, a quiet waiting room *(Warteraum)* that's open to anybody, and the DB Lounge for first-class ticket holders only (no rail passes).

If you get lost in the underground maze of subway corridors, to find the train station, follow signs for *DB* (Deutsche Bahn) to surface successfully.

Munich's Bus Station: The central bus station (ZOB) is by the Hackerbrücke S-Bahn station, one stop from the train station (www.muenchen-zob.de).

HELPFUL HINTS

Tourist Information (TI): Munich has two TIs (www.muenchen.de): At **Marienplatz,** below the glockenspiel (Mon-Fri 9:00-19:00, Sat 9:00-16:00, Sun 10:00-14:00), and in front of the **main train station**—with your back to the tracks, walk through the central hall, step outside, and turn right (Mon-Sat 9:00-20:00, Sun 10:00-18:00).

Both TIs have brochures, sell concert tickets, book hotel rooms, and answer your sightseeing questions. Make a point to pick up the free *In München* entertainment schedule (in German, organized by date) and pay extra for their city map (€0.40), which is better than the free maps hotels give out. The TIs also sell Gray Line bus tours of the city (see page 177), and bus tours to nearby castles like Neuschwanstein (see page 116).

For general info on Bavaria, try www.bavaria.us.

EurAide: Also at the train station (opposite track 21, inside the *Reisezentrum* travel center), these helpful folks dole out free advice on train travel and day trips in clear American English. They sell train tickets, reservations, and *couchettes* at no extra charge. They also sell (cash-only) tickets for city walking tours, Gray Line bus tours of the city, and Gray Line tours to Neuschwanstein. If the EurAide line's too long, at least pick up their extremely informative *Inside Track* newsletter, which probably answers most of your questions anyway (open May-Oct Mon-Fri 8:30-20:00, Sat 8:30-14:00, closed Sun; off-season Mon-Fri 10:00-19:00, closed Sat-Sun and Jan-Feb, www.euraide.com).

Hurdling the Language Barrier: Most Germans and Austrians, especially those in cities and in the tourist trade, speak at least some English. Still, you'll get more smiles using a few German pleasantries. It's polite to greet your fellow travelers in the hotel breakfast room in the morning *("Gute Morgen")* and greet small shop owners as you enter *(Guten Tag)*. Learn

Buy transit tix from multilingual machines.

What language barrier?

please *(Bitte),* thank you *(Danke),* and yes and no *(ja/nein).* Goodbye is *Auf Wiedersehen,* and you toast someone by raising your glass—*Prost!*

⚙ To learn a few more German phrases, see page 179.

Pedestrian Safety: As Munich is geared heavily for biking, pedestrians need to pay close attention to signs showing which part of the sidewalk is designated for pedestrians and which for cyclists. Also, Munich's trams can be dangerous for pedestrians unused to these silent-moving vehicles.

Time Zones: Germany's time zone is six/nine hours ahead of the east/west coasts of the US.

Business Hours: Most shops are open Monday through Saturday from about 9:00 until 18:00-20:00 (some close by 17:00 on Sat). Even Munich—a city of a million people—is mostly closed up on Sunday. (Need something? Try the train station.) Banks are generally open weekdays from 9:00 to 15:00 (or sometimes later). You'll find a few small late-night grocery stores, especially near train stations. Businesses are often closed on Catholic holidays.

Festivals: Oktoberfest lasts around two weeks, starting on the third Saturday in September and usually ending on the first Sunday in October (www.oktoberfest.de). The same fairgrounds also host a Spring Festival (*Frühlingsfestival,* two weeks in late April-early May, www.fruehlingsfest-muenchen.de) as well as Tollwood, an artsy, multicultural, alternative Christmas market (late Nov-Dec, www.tollwood.de).

Watt's Up? Europe's electrical system is 220 volts, instead of North America's 110 volts. You'll need an adapter plug with two round prongs, sold inexpensively at travel stores in the US. Most newer electronics (such

Tipping

Tipping in Germany isn't as generous as it is in the US. To tip a taxi driver, round up to the next euro (for a €4.70 fare, give €5). For longer rides, figure about 5-10 percent. At hotels, if you let the porter carry your luggage, tip a euro for each bag. For sit-down service in a restaurant, it's common to tip 10 percent after a good meal. But if you order your food or drinks at a counter, don't tip.

as mobile devices, laptops, hair dryers, and battery chargers) convert automatically, so you won't need a separate converter.

Numbers and Stumblers: What Americans call the second floor of a building is the first floor in Europe. Europeans write dates as day/month/year. Commas are decimal points and vice versa—a dollar and half is 1,50, and there are 5.280 feet in a mile. Germany uses the metric system: A kilogram is 2.2 pounds; a liter is about a quart; and a kilometer is six-tenths of a mile. Temperature is measured in Celsius: 0°C = 32°F. To roughly convert Celsius to Fahrenheit, double the number and add 30.

Internet Access: There's free Wi-Fi on Marienplatz (connect to "M-WLAN network," then click to accept terms). If you need a computer, there are a number of hole-in-the-wall Internet/call centers near the train station.

Bookstore: Hugendubel towers above Marienplatz with a good selection of English books, comfy nooks for reading, and a view café (Mon-Sat 9:30-20:00, closed Sun, Marienplatz 22, tel. 089/3075-7575).

Public Toilets: Though there are few public WCs, by law, any place serving beer must let the public (whether or not they're customers) use the toilets.

Laundry: Waschcenter is a 10-minute walk from the train station. It costs about €10 to wash and dry a load yourself, or €12 drop-off service (self-service daily 7:00-23:00, drop-off Mon-Sat 10:00-20:00, Sun 11:00-18:00, Paul-Heyse-Strasse 21, near intersection with Landwehrstrasse, Theresienwiese is the closest U-Bahn station, mobile 0171-734-2094).

Great City Views: Downtown Munich's best city viewpoints (all described elsewhere in this book) are from the towers of St. Peter's Church (stairs only), New Town Hall (elevator), and the Frauenkirche (towers may be closed for renovation).

What's with Monaco? People walking around with guidebooks to Monaco aren't lost. "Monaco di Baviera" means "Munich" in *Italiano*.

GETTING AROUND MUNICH

Much of Munich is walkable. But—given that the city is laced by many trams, buses, and the subway—it's worth learning the system and considering getting a day pass. Public transit also makes it super-easy to access sights outside the historic core, such as Dachau or Nymphenburg Palace.

By Public Transit

The transit system includes trams (a.k.a. streetcars), buses, and a subway system of U-Bahn (subway) and S-Bahn (faster suburban) trains.

Ticket Options: The entire transit system (subway/bus/tram) works on the same tickets.

• A one-zone **regular ticket** *(Einzelfahrkarte)* costs €2.60 and is good for three hours in one direction, including changes and stops. A one-zone ticket will get you to most of Munich's main tourist sights, except for Dachau (green zone) and the airport (orange zone).

• **All-day passes** can be a great deal. The €6 *Single-Tageskarte* covers the white/inner zone. The *Single-Tageskarte XXL* also includes Dachau (€8.10). The *Gesamtnetz* pass—a.k.a. the "Airport-City-Day-Ticket"—covers all four zones and gets you to the airport (€11.70).

• **All-day small-group passes** are an even better deal for couples and families—they cover all public transportation for up to five adults. A *Partner-Tageskarte* for the white/inner zone costs €11.20. The *Partner-Tageskarte XXL,* which includes Dachau, costs €14.20. The *Gesamtnetz* version, including the airport, costs €21.30. Do the math, and you'll realize these passes can be a great deal, even for only two people. The only catch is that your group has to travel together.

• For longer stays, consider a **three-day pass** (€15/single, €25.90/small-group, white/inner zone only, does not include transportation to Dachau). All-day and multi-day passes are valid until 6:00 the following morning.

• The **City Tour Card**—a transit day-pass that includes a few sightseeing discounts—is not worth the mental overhead for most people, but you can check out the specifics at www.citytourcard-muenchen.com.

Buying Tickets: Transit tickets are sold at TIs, at booths in the subway, and at any ticket machine that has the MVV logo. Machines take coins and €5 and €10 bills; newer ones take PIN-enabled credit cards, too. Start the transaction by choosing "English," then by pressing "Transit Association-MVV," which displays the array of tickets and passes.

Using the System: To get your bearings (on any tram, bus, U-Bahn, or S-Bahn), you'll want to know the end-of-the-line stop in the direction you're heading. The lines are known by their number (U-1 or Tram #17 or Bus #100) and by their end-of-the-line stops. So, to find the right platform, follow the posted signs: a sign saying *Richtung: Marienplatz,* for example, means that that particular subway, bus, or tram is traveling in the direction *(Richtung)* of Marienplatz.

You must validate your ticket or pass by getting it stamped. (However, tickets and passes bought from ticket-vending machines come pre-stamped, and day-passes only need to be stamped the first time you use them.) For the subway, punch your ticket in the blue machine *before* going down to the platform. For buses and trams, the stamping machine is on board. Plainclothes ticket-checkers enforce this honor system, rewarding freeloaders with stiff €40 fines. On the trams, rookies miss stops because they fail to open the door. Push buttons, pull latches—do whatever it takes.

Handy Lines: Several subway lines, trams, and buses are especially convenient for tourists.

• All the main S-Bahn lines (S-1 through S-8) run east-west along the main tourist axis between the Hauptbahnhof, Marienplatz, and the Ostbahnhof. For travel within the city center, just find the platform for lines S-1 through S-8. One track *(Gleis)* will be headed east to the Ostbahnhof, the other west to the Hauptbahnhof. Hop on any train going your direction.

• The U-3 goes to Olympic Park and the BMW sights.

• The S-2 goes to Dachau.

• Bus #100 is useful for getting to the museum quarter and the English Garden.

• Tram #17 goes to Nymphenburg Palace.

For more information, visit the transit customer-service center at Marienplatz (Mon-Sat only, go down stairs by Beck's department store), call 0800-344-226-600 (Mon-Fri only), or visit www.mvv-muenchen.de.

By Taxi

Taxis are honest and professional, but expensive (about €12 between the Hauptbahnhof and Marienplatz) and generally unnecessary. Call 089/21610 for a taxi. Private driver Johann Fayoumi is reliable and speaks English (€70/hour, mobile 0174-183-8473, www.firstclasslimousines.de).

By Bike

Level, compact, and with plenty of bike paths, Munich feels made for those on two wheels. Veteran urban bikers could easily use a bike here as their major transportation. The less daring might still enjoy a short joy ride or a group bike tour.

Bike Rental Shops: These two bike rental places provide helmets, maps, and route advice, and also offer bike tours: **Radius Tours** (*Rad* means "bike" in German) is in the train station by track 32 (€3/hour or €17/24 hours for basic bikes, give credit-card number as deposit; April-Oct daily 8:30-19:00, May-Aug until 20:00; closed Nov-March; tel. 089/543-487-7730, www.radiustours.com). **Mike's Bike Tours** is around the corner from the rear entrance to the Hofbräuhaus (€6 plus €2/hour, €16/day, daily mid-April-early Oct 10:00-20:00, shorter hours off-season, open by appointment mid-Nov-Feb, Bräuhausstrasse 10, tel. 089/2554-3987, www.mikesbiketours.com).

Self-Guided Isar River Bike Ride: Here's an easy, scenic ride you can do on your own. Munich's river, lined by a gorgeous park, leads bikers into the pristine countryside in just a few minutes. Start on the eastern edge of downtown—from the English Garden or Deutsches Museum (closest bike rental is Mike's Bike Tours). Follow the riverside bike path south (upstream) along the east (left) bank. You can't get lost. Just stay

Trams take you where the U-Bahn doesn't.

Covering the sights by bike, with a guide

on the lovely bike path. It crosses the river after a while, passing tempting little *Biergartens* and lots of Bavarians having their brand of fun—including gangs enjoying Munich's famous river party rafts. Go as far as you like, then retrace your route to get home.

Self-Guided Ride to Nymphenburg, Olympic Park, and BMW: Here's another great day on a bike: From the train station, take the bike path out Arnulfstrasse, pedaling out to Nymphenburg Palace. Then head to Olympic Park and the BMW sights, and finish at the English Garden (for the late-afternoon or early-evening scene) before returning to the center.

Bike Tours: If you prefer riding in a group with a guide, this is a pleasant way to see the city sights. For around €20-25 (including bike rental), you ride a 3.5-hour circuit, pausing here and there for the guide to point things out, and maybe stopping for a (buy-your-own) lunch break. No need to reserve, just show up. Tours only go from around mid-March to mid-November, so confirm times in advance. Try Radius Tours (tours depart from train station track 32, www.radiustours.com); Mike's Bike Tours (departs from Marienplatz's Old Town Hall, tel. 089/2554-3987, www.mikesbiketours.com); Munich Walk (departs from Marienplatz TI, www.munichwalktours.de); or Lenny's Bike Tours (for young backpacker crowd, departs from Marienplatz fish fountain, www.discovermunichnow.com).

COMMUNICATING

The easiest (if not cheapest) way to stay connected while on the road—planning your sightseeing, contacting hotels, and staying in touch back home—is to bring your own mobile device (phone, smartphone, tablet, or laptop) and keep your home carrier. But you can also do fine bringing no device at all, relying only on your hotel's public computer, Internet cafés, and public phones. Read on for more details and budget alternatives. For more on all of these options, see www.ricksteves.com/phoning.

Using the Internet: Traveling with a mobile device gives you on-the-go access to the Internet and travel-oriented apps. The Munich TI has a free downloadable app for tourists on its website (www.muenchen.de). CityMaps2Go has free street maps that can be used offline. You can make free or cheap phone calls using Skype, Google Talk, or Facetime.

To avoid sky-high fees for data roaming, disable data roaming entirely, and only go online when you have Wi-Fi (e.g., at your hotel or in a

One key to Munich's livability is its combination of traditional culture with modern convenience.

café). Or you could sign up for an international data plan for the duration of your trip: $30 typically buys about 100 megabytes—enough to view 100 websites or send/receive 1,000 emails.

Most hotels offer some form of free or cheap Internet access—either a shared computer in the lobby or Wi-Fi in the room. Otherwise, your hotelier can point you to the nearest Internet café (or try the train station neighborhood). You'll also find Wi-Fi hotspots at many cafés (Wi-Fi is sometimes called "WLAN" in Germany.)

Making Phone Calls: Many US mobile phones work in Europe. Expect to pay around $1.50 a minute for phone calls and 30 cents per text message (less if you sign up for an international calling plan with your service provider). If you plan to make a lot of calls, consider outfitting your phone with a European SIM card—that is, temporarily sign up with a European carrier. (For more on how SIM cards work, see www.ricksteves.com/phoning).

It's easy to buy a phone in Europe, which costs more up front but is cheaper by the call. You'll find mobile-phone stores selling cheap phones (for as little as $20 plus minutes) and SIM cards, at the airport and train stations, and throughout Munich.

Dialing Tips: To call Germany from the US or Canada: Dial 011 (our international access code) + 49 (Germany's country code) + the local number, without the initial zero. To call Germany from a European country: Dial 00 (Europe's international access code) + 49 followed by the local number, without the initial zero. To call within Germany: If you're dialing locally, just dial the number, without its area code. If you're dialing from outside the area code, you must include the three-digit code (which, in Germany, always starts with a zero). To call from Germany to another country: Dial 00, the country code (for example, 1 for the US or Canada), then the area code and number. If you're calling European countries whose phone numbers begin with 0, you'll usually have to omit that 0 when you dial. If you're calling from Europe using your US mobile phone, you may need to dial as if you're calling from the US.

Phoning Inexpensively: Here's a budget alternative if you don't carry a mobile phone: Buy an international phone card (€5). This give you pennies-per-minute rates on international calls, decent rates for calls within Austria, and can even be used from your hotel phone or a European mobile phone. Buy cards at newsstands, electronics stores, and Internet cafés. When using an international phone card, you always must dial the area

Useful Contacts

Police: Tel. 112
Emergency Medical Assistance: Tel. 112
US Embassy in Berlin: Pariser Platz 2, tel. 030/83050, www.germany.usembassy.gov
Canadian Embassy in Berlin: Leipziger Platz 17, tel. 030/203-120, www.germany.gc.ca
U.S. Consulate General Munich: Königinstraße 5, tel. 030/203-120, www.munich.usconsulate.gov
Collect Calls to the US: Tel. 0800-225-5288 (press 0 or stay on the line for an English-speaking operator)
Directory Assistance Within Germany: Tel. 11833
International Directory Assistance: Tel. 11834

code, even if you're calling across the street. Calling from your hotel room without a phone card can be a rip-off—ask your hotelier about their rates before you dial. Since German hotels don't charge for receiving calls, it can be more affordable to have someone from the US call you.

SIGHTSEEING TIPS

Hours: Hours of sights can change unexpectedly, so confirm the latest times at a TI, at the sight's website, or at the general Munich website (www.muenchen.de). Many sights stop admitting people 30–60 minutes before closing time, and guards start shooing people out before the actual closing time, so don't save the best for last.

What to Expect: Important sights might have metal detectors or conduct bag searches that will slow your entry. Many sights require you to check any bag bigger than a purse, and sometimes even purses. Museum lockers are free, but be prepared to have a €1 or €2 coin for deposit.

Photos and videos are normally allowed, but flashes or tripods usually are not. Many sights offer guided tours and rent audioguides (€4–7). Expect changes—artwork can be in restoration or on tour. Most have an on-site café.

Discounts: Those under age 18 (under 19 in Austria) get in free to state-run museums and sights. Some sights have discounts for students (with International Student Identity Cards, www.isic.org). Senior discounts are generally only for EU residents, but it's worth asking.

Free Rick Steves Audio Tours: I've produced free audio tours of the Munich City Walk and Salzburg Old Town Walk. Download them to your mobile device via the Rick Steves Audio Europe smartphone app, www.ricksteves.com/audioeurope, iTunes, or Google Play.

Advance Tickets and Sightseeing Cards

For the sights in Munich and Salzburg, you don't need advance tickets to avoid lines, even during peak season. However, at Neuschwanstein Castle, consider reservations between April and October, and definitely in July-August (see page 113).

Mehrtagesticket: This 14-day combo-ticket (€24, or €40 family/partner pass) covers admission to dozens of Bavarian palaces, including the Munich Residenz, Nymphenburg Palace, and Neuschwanstein Castle (but not Hohenschwangau Castle). The pass will pay for itself if you're seeing even two of those three sights (and the family pass is an even better deal), so it's definitely worth considering. Buy the ticket at any participating sight (details at www.schloesser.bayern.de).

THEFT AND EMERGENCIES

Theft: While violent crime is rare, thieves (mainly pickpockets) thrive near famous monuments, on public transportation, at places of drunkenness, in hostels, or anywhere crowds press together. Be alert to the possibility of theft, even when you're absorbed in the wonder and newness of Munich. Smartphones are thief-magnets. I keep my valuables—passport, credit cards, crucial documents, and large amounts of cash—in a money belt that I tuck under my beltline. Dial 112 for police help. If you lose your debit/credit cards, call the numbers on page 161. To replace a passport, file the police report, then call your embassy to make an appointment.

Medical Help: Dial 112 for a medical emergency. Most doctors speak English. For minor ailments, do as the Germans do and first visit a pharmacy (*Apotheke)*, where qualified technicians routinely diagnose and prescribe. There's a pharmacy inside the New Town Hall on Marienplatz (Mon-Sat 9:00-20:00). Otherwise, ask your hotelier for assistance.

ACTIVITIES

Shopping

Munich, with its many pedestrian streets, feels purpose-built for browsing and window-shopping. You won't need a guidebook to find plenty of stores selling beer steins and Mad-King-Ludwig fridge magnets. But Munich is also known for its elegant, high-end goods.

Shopping Neighborhoods: Look no further than the glamorous area around **Marienplatz.** Here you'll find the major department stores (typically open Mon-Sat 9:30-20:00). Ludwig Beck, a 150-year-old local institution, is too expensive to actually buy anything in (€200 for a pair of jeans) but fun to browse. A slight notch down is Karstadt, followed by the mid-range Kaufhof (with a wide selection of practical goods for the traveler in need), and the cheap clothing store C&A. Strolling the pedestrian-only **Kaufingerstrasse** gives an array of global chains and local favorites. **Weinstrasse,** the street heading north from Marienplatz, leads pleasantly to Marienhof with its great-for-grazing Dallmayr Delicatessen (see page 31). Farther north on Weinstrasse (which becomes Theatinerstrasse) is the delightful **Fünf Höfe Passage** shopping mall, an architectural sight in itself (open Mon-Fri 10:00-19:00, Sat 10:00-18:00, closed Sun; see page 31). **Maximilianstrasse,** an arcaded shopping street since the 1850s, has Munich's most exclusive shops (see page 34).

Bavarian Souvenirs: For **basic souvenirs** (like that stein you promised your uncle), try the gift shops on Kaufingerstrasse (near St. Michael's Church) or by the Hofbräuhaus. For more unusual gifts, there's the amusing Servus Heimat shop (at the Munich City Museum, see page 82, www. servusheimat.com). **Dirndls and lederhosen,** which many locals still wear on special occasions, don't come cheap. Find traditional clothing (*Trachten* in German) at the high-end Loden-Frey Verkaufshaus department store (a block west of Marienplatz at Maffeistrasse 7, tel. 089/210-390, www.loden-frey.com). Less expensive is Angermaier Trachten (near the Viktualienmarkt, Rosental 10, tel. 089/2300-0199, www.trachten-angermaier.de). For classic wooden **toys and puppets** there's Obletter (Karlsplatz 11, tel. 089/5508-9510). Find **porcelain** dinnerware and figurines at the Nymphenburg Porcelain Store (Odeonsplatz 1, tel. 089/282-428, www.nymphenburg.com). If you just need **practical goods,** try the multi-purpose Kaufhof department store near Marienplatz. If you're looking for a used cell phone or exotic groceries, the area south of the train station fits the bill.

Getting a VAT Refund: If you purchase more than €75.01 worth of goods at a single store, you may be eligible to get a refund of the 20 percent Value-Added Tax (VAT). Have the store fill out the paperwork, then get it stamped at the airport by Customs and processed by a VAT refund company (e.g., Global Blue or Premier Tax/Travelex; you'll find Global Blue in the Munich airport departure area). Get more details from your merchant or see ricksteves.com/vat.

Customs for American Shoppers: You are allowed to take home $800 worth of items per person duty-free, once every 30 days. You can also bring in duty-free a liter of alcohol. As for food, you can take home many processed and packaged foods (e.g., vacuum-packed cheeses, chocolate, mustard) but no fresh produce or meats. Any liquid-containing foods must be packed in checked luggage, a potential recipe for disaster. To check customs rules and duty rates, visit www.cbp.gov.

Nightlife

For most tourists—and many locals—a night on the town in Munich means going to a beer hall or beer garden, ordering a wurst and sauerkraut, hefting a stein, and swaying along to an oompah band. On a balmy evening under the stars or in a cozy cellar with friendly natives, it's hard to beat that kind of scene. You'll find plenty of suggestions for beer halls and beer gardens in the Eating chapter (see page 99). Other Munchners prefer to

Lederhosen are classy and pricey.

Munich nightlife—theater, music, and beer

Practicalities

simply stroll the streets around Marienplatz, window-shopping, enjoying an *eis,* and listening to a street-corner string quartet.

Here are a few other nightlife alternatives to the beer-and-oompah scene:

Music and Dance: Ballet and opera fans can check the schedule at the **Bayerisch Staatsoper,** centrally located right by the Residenz. Because of high demand, book at least a month ahead—seats range from €13 to very pricey (Max-Joseph-Platz 2, tel. 089/2185-1920, www. bayerische.staatsoper.de). The **Hotel Bayerischerhof's** night club has live music—major jazz acts plus pop/soul/disco—in a posh, dress-up, expensive setting (Promenadeplatz 2, tel. 089/212-0994, www.bayerischer hof.de). For familiar Broadway-style musicals (though most are performed in German), try the **Deutsches Theatre,** conveniently located near my train-station hotels (Schwanthalerstrasse 13, tel. 089/5523-4120, www. deutsches-theater.de).

Pubs and Clubs: If you just want to explore an untouristed area known for its nightlife—both gay and straight—get out your map and find **Gärtnerplatz** (a 30-minute walk due south of Marienplatz, bus #52 from Marienplatz, or U-1 or U2 to Fraunhoferstrasse). Near the Viktualienmarkt is a quirky-but-fun pub called **Heilig-Geist-Stüberl** ("Holy Ghost Pub"). This funky, retro little hole-in-the-wall has plenty of locals and a time-warp 1980s interior that's like stepping into an alcoholic cuckoo clock (nightly until 22:00, Heiliggeiststrasse 1).

Late-Night Museums: The art museums in the Museum Quarter are open late one night a week. See the Daily Reminder on page 8 for a day-by-day rundown.

Guided Tours
Guided Group Walking Tours: Two reliable companies with knowledgeable guides give a two-hour once-over of the main sights of central Munich for around €14. Reservations aren't necessary; just show up. **Radius Tours** (www.radiustours.com) leaves daily at 10:00 from the train station by track 32. **Munich Walk** (www.munichwalktours.de) leaves daily at 10:45 from the Marienplatz TI. Both companies also offer themed tours, such as the birth of Nazism or food-tasting tours—see their websites. In Munich, numerous companies advertise "free" guided tours, but the quality is unpredictable and they expect a tip (€5-10, if it's worthwhile).

See the sights on a hop-on, hop-off bus… …or by joining a guided walking tour.

Pub Crawls: These are understandably popular. For around €25-30, you meet your group around 18:30 for a 3.5-hour tour of several beer halls, where you learn a bit of brewing history, and sample local food and drink. No need to reserve for these tours, just show up. Try Radius Tours or Munich Walks (mentioned earlier) or the Size Matters Beer Tour (www.sizemattersbeertour.de).

Hop-on, Hop-off Bus Tours: These give a drive-by once-over of the city's major landmarks (Marienplatz, Karlsplatz, the Museum Quarter) while you listen to a canned commentary. Your ticket's good all day, so you can hop on and off to sightsee as you go. Gray Line Tours leaves from the Karstadt department store directly across from the train station. Choose from their basic, one-hour "Express Circle" (€15, 3/hour, 9:40-18:00) or the 2.5-hour "Grand Circle" that also includes Nymphenburg Palace and the BMW-Welt/Museum (€15, hourly 9:40-16:00)—it's a handy way to reach these outlying sights. Just show up and pay the driver (tel. 089/5490-7560, www.sightseeing-munich.com).

Private Guides: Though pricey, these can be a great value if you're splitting the cost between several people. I've had great days with two good guides: Georg Reichlmayr (€165/3 hours, tel. 08131/86800, mobile 0170-341-6384, www.muenchen-stadtfuehrung.de) and Monika Hank (€115/2 hours, €135/3 hours, tel. 089/311-4819, mobile 0172-547-8123, monika.hank@web.de).

Bike Tours: See page 169.

RESOURCES FROM RICK STEVES

This Pocket guide is one of dozens of titles in my series of guidebooks on European travel. I also produce a public television series, *Rick Steves' Europe*, and a public radio show, *Travel with Rick Steves*. My website, www.ricksteves.com, offers a wealth of free travel resources, including videos and podcasts of my shows, audio tours of Europe's great sights, travel forums, guidebook updates, and information on European rail—plus an online travel store and specifics on our tours of Europe. If you want to be my virtual travel partner, follow me on Facebook and Twitter as I share my latest news and on-the-road spills, thrills, and insights. If you have feedback on this book, please fill out the survey at www.ricksteves.com/feedback. It helps us and fellow travelers.

German Survival Phrases

When using the phonetics, pronounce ī as the long I sound in "light."
Bolded syllables are stressed.

English	German	Phonetics
Good day.	**Guten Tag.**	GOO-tehn tahg
Do you speak English?	**Sprechen Sie Englisch?**	SHPREHKH-ehn zee EHGN-lish
Yes. / No.	**Ja. / Nein.**	yah / nīn
I (don't) understand.	**Ich verstehe (nicht).**	ikh fehr-SHTAY-heh (nikht)
Please.	**Bitte.**	BIT-teh
Thank you.	**Danke.**	DAHNG-keh
I'm sorry.	**Es tut mir leid.**	ehs toot meer līt
Excuse me.	**Entschuldigung.**	ehnt-SHOOL-dig-oong
(No) problem.	**(Kein) Problem.**	(kīn) proh-BLAYM
(Very) good.	**(Sehr) gut.**	(zehr) goot
Goodbye.	**Auf Wiedersehen.**	owf VEE-der-zayn
one / two	**eins / zwei**	īns / tsvī
three / four	**drei / vier**	drī / feer
five / six	**fünf / sechs**	fewnf / zehkhs
seven / eight	**sieben / acht**	ZEE-behn / ahkht
nine / ten	**neun / zehn**	noyn / tsayn
How much is it?	**Wieviel kostet das?**	VEE-feel KOHS-teht dahs
Write it?	**Schreiben?**	SHRĪ-behn
Is it free?	**Ist es umsonst?**	ist ehs oom-ZOHNST
Included?	**Inklusive?**	in-kloo-ZEE-veh
Where can I buy / find...?	**Wo kann ich kaufen / finden...?**	voh kahn ikh KOW-fehn / FIN-dehn
I'd like / We'd like...	**Ich hätte gern / Wir hätten gern...**	ikh HEH-teh gehrn / veer HEH-tehn gehrn
...a room.	**...ein Zimmer.**	īn TSIM-mer
...a ticket to ___.	**...eine Fahrkarte nach ___.**	Ī-neh FAR-kar-teh nahkh
Is it possible?	**Ist es möglich?**	ist ehs MUR-glikh
Where is...?	**Wo ist...?**	voh ist
...the train station	**...der Bahnhof**	dehr BAHN-hohf
...the bus station	**...der Busbahnhof**	dehr BOOS-bahn-hohf
...the tourist information office	**...das Touristen-informations-büro**	dahs too-RIS-tehn-in-for-maht-see-OHNS-BEW-roh
...the toilet	**...die Toilette**	dee toh-LEH-teh
men	**Herren**	HEHR-rehn
women	**Damen**	DAH-mehn
left / right	**links / rechts**	links / rehkhts
straight	**geradeaus**	geh-RAH-deh-OWS
What time does this open / close?	**Um wieviel Uhr wird hier geöffnet / geschlossen?**	oom VEE-feel oor veerd heer geh-URF-neht / geh-SHLOH-sehn
At what time?	**Um wieviel Uhr?**	oom VEE-feel oor
Just a moment.	**Moment.**	moh-MEHNT
now / soon / later	**jetzt / bald / später**	yehtst / bahld / SHPAY-ter
today / tomorrow	**heute / morgen**	HOY-teh / MOR-gehn

In the Restaurant

English	German	Pronunciation
I'd like / We'd like...	Ich hätte gern / Wir hätten gern...	ikh HEH-teh gehrn / veer HEH-tehn gehrn
...a reservation for...	...eine Reservierung für...	Ī-neh reh-zer-FEER-oong fewr
...a table for one / two.	...einen Tisch für eine Person / zwei Personen.	Ī-nehn tish fewr Ī-neh pehr- zohn / tsvī pehr-zohnehn
Non-smoking.	Nichtraucher.	NIKHT-rowkh-er
Is this seat free?	Ist hier frei?	ist heer frī
Menu (in English), please.	Speisekarte (auf Englisch), bitte.	SHPĪ-zeh-kar-teh (owf EHNG-lish) BIT-teh
service (not) included	Trinkgeld (nicht) inklusive	TRINK-gehlt (nikht) in-kloo-ZEE-veh
cover charge	Eintritt	ĪN-trit
to go	zum Mitnehmen	tsoom MIT-nay-mehn
with / without	mit / ohne	mit / OH-neh
and / or	und / oder	oont / OH-der
menu (of the day)	(Tages-) Karte	(TAH-gehs-) KAR-teh
set meal for tourists	Touristenmenü	too-RIS-tehn-meh-NEW
specialty of the house	Spezialität des Hauses	SHPAYT-see-ah-lee-TAYT dehs HOW-zehs
appetizers	Vorspeise	FOR-shpī-zeh
bread / cheese	Brot / Käse	broht / KAY-zeh
sandwich	Sandwich	ZAHND-vich
soup	Suppe	ZUP-peh
salad	Salat	zah-LAHT
meat	Fleisch	flīsh
poultry	Geflügel	geh-FLEW-gehl
fish	Fisch	fish
seafood	Meeresfrüchte	MEH-rehs-FREWKH-teh
fruit	Obst	ohpst
vegetables	Gemüse	geh-MEW-zeh
dessert	Nachspeise	NAHKH-shpī-zeh
mineral water	Mineralwasser	min-eh-RAHL-vah-ser
tap water	Leitungswasser	LĪ-toongs-vah-ser
milk	Milch	milkh
(orange) juice	(Orangen-) Saft	(oh-RAHN-zhehn-) zahft
coffee / tea	Kaffee / Tee	kah-FAY / tay
wine	Wein	vīn
red / white	rot / weiß	roht / vīs
glass / bottle	Glas / Flasche	glahs / FLAH-sheh
beer	Bier	beer
Cheers!	Prost!	prohst
More. / Another.	Mehr. / Noch eins.	mehr / nohkh īns
The same.	Das gleiche.	dahs GLĪKH-eh
Bill, please.	Rechnung, bitte.	REHKH-noong BIT-teh
tip	Trinkgeld	TRINK-gehlt
Delicious!	Lecker!	LEHK-er

For more user-friendly German phrases, check out *Rick Steves' German Phrase Book and Dictionary* or *Rick Steves' French, Italian & German Phrase Book*.

INDEX

Index

Index

Start your trip at

Our website enhances this book and turns

Explore Europe

At ricksteves.com you can browse through thousands of articles, videos, photos and radio interviews, plus find a wealth of money-saving travel tips for planning your dream trip. And with our mobile-friendly website, you can easily access all this great travel information anywhere you go.

TV Shows

Preview the places you'll visit by watching entire half-hour episodes of Rick Steves' Europe (choose from all 100 shows) on-demand, for free.

ricksteves.com

your travel dreams into affordable reality

Radio Interviews

Enjoy ready access to Rick's vast library of radio interviews covering  travel tips and cultural insights that relate specifically to your Europe travel plans.

Travel Forums

Learn, ask, share! Our online community of savvy travelers is a great resource for first-time travelers to Europe, as well as seasoned pros. You'll find forums on each country, plus travel tips and restaurant/hotel reviews. You can even ask one of our well-traveled staff to chime in with an opinion.

Travel News

Subscribe to our free Travel News e-newsletter, and get monthly updates from Rick on what's happening in Europe.

Audio Europe™

Rick's Free Travel App

Get your FREE Rick Steves Audio Europe™ app to enjoy...

- Dozens of self-guided tours of Europe's top museums, sights and historic walks
- Hundreds of tracks filled with cultural insights and sightseeing tips from Rick's radio interviews
- All organized into handy geographic playlists
- For Apple and Android

With Rick whispering in your ear, Europe gets even better.

Find out more at ricksteves.com

Pack Light and Right

Gear up for your next adventure at ricksteves.com

Light Luggage

Pack light and right with Rick Steves' affordable, custom-designed rolling carry-on bags, backpacks, day packs and shoulder bags.

Accessories

From packing cubes to moneybelts and beyond, Rick has personally selected the travel goodies that will help your trip go smoother.

Shop at ricksteves.com

Rick Steves has

Experience maximum Europe

Save time and energy

This guidebook is your independent-travel toolkit. But for all it delivers, it's still up to you to devote the time and energy it takes to manage the preparation and logistics that are essential for a happy trip. If that's a hassle, there's a solution.

Rick Steves Tours

A Rick Steves tour takes you to Europe's most interesting places with great guides and small groups

great tours, too!

with minimum stress

of 28 or less. We follow Rick's favorite itineraries, ride in comfy buses, stay in family-run hotels, and bring you intimately close to the Europe you've traveled so far to see. Most importantly, we take away the logistical headaches so you can focus on the fun.

Join the fun

This year we'll take thousands of free-spirited travelers—nearly half of them repeat customers—along with us on four dozen different itineraries, from Ireland to Italy to Istanbul. Is a Rick Steves tour the right fit for your travel dreams? Find out at ricksteves.com, where you can also request Rick's latest tour catalog.

Europe is best experienced with happy travel partners. We hope you can join us.

See our itineraries at ricksteves.com

A Guide for Every Trip

BEST OF GUIDES

Full color easy-to-scan format, focusing on Europe's most popular destinations and sights.

Best of France
Best of Germany
Best of England
Best of Europe
Best of Ireland
Best of Italy
Best of Spain

COMPREHENSIVE GUIDES

City, country, and regional guides with detailed coverage for a multi-week trip exploring iconic sights and more.

Amsterdam & the Netherlands
Barcelona
Belgium: Bruges, Brussels,
  Antwerp & Ghent
Berlin
Budapest
Croatia & Slovenia

Eastern Europe
England
Florence & Tuscany
France
Germany
Great Britain
Greece: Athens
  & the Peloponnese
Iceland
Ireland
Istanbul
Italy
London
Paris
Portugal
Prague & the Czech Republic
Provence & the French Riviera
Rome
Scandinavia
Scotland
Spain
Switzerland
Venice
Vienna, Salzburg & Tirol

Rick Steves guidebooks are published by Avalon Travel,
an imprint of Perseus Books, a Hachette Book Group company.

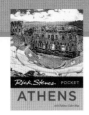

POCKET GUIDES

Amsterdam
Athens
Barcelona
Florence
Italy's Cinque Terre
London

Munich & Salzburg
Paris
Prague
Rome
Venice
Vienna

SNAPSHOT GUIDES

Focused single-destination coverage.

Basque Country: Spain & France
Copenhagen & the Best of Denmark
Dublin
Dubrovnik
Edinburgh
Hill Towns of Central Italy
Krakow, Warsaw & Gdansk
Lisbon
Loire Valley
Madrid & Toledo
Milan & the Italian Lakes District
Naples & the Amalfi Coast
Northern Ireland
Normandy
Norway
Reykjavik
Sevilla, Granada & Southern Spain
St. Petersburg, Helsinki & Tallinn
Stockholm

CRUISE PORTS GUIDES

Reference for cruise ports of call.

Mediterranean Cruise Ports
Northern European Cruise Ports

TRAVEL SKILLS & CULTURE

Europe 101
European Christmas
European Easter
European Festivals
Europe Through the Back Door
Postcards from Europe
Travel as a Political Act

PHRASE BOOKS & DICTIONARIES

French
French, Italian & German
German
Italian
Portuguese
Spanish

PLANNING MAPS

Britain, Ireland & London
Europe
France & Paris
Germany, Austria & Switzerland
Ireland
Italy
Spain & Portugal

Rick Steves books are available from your favorite bookseller.
Many guides are available as ebooks.

PHOTO CREDITS

Cover
Left photo: Antique sign on Getreidegasse in old city, Salzburg © Paul Beinssen/ Getty Images
Right photo: Odeonsplatz, Munich © Dominic Arizona Bonuccelli

Introduction
Pages 1, 2 left, 2 right, 3: © Dominic Bonuccelli

Munich City Walk
Pages 13, 28 left, 32, 33 right, 35, 38: © Dominic Bonuccelli
Page 36: © Everett Collection Historical / Alamy

Munich Residenz Tour
Pages 39, 41 left, 47: © Dominic Bonuccelli

Dachau Concentration Camp Memorial Tour
Page: 77: © DIZ Muenchen GmbH, Sueddeutsche Zeitung Photo / Alamy

More Munich Sights
Pages 83 left, 84: © Dominic Bonuccelli

Sleeping
Pages 91, 98: © Dominic Bonuccelli

Eating
Pages 99, 102 left, 102 right, 104 left, 106: © Dominic Bonuccelli

Neuschwanstein Castle and a Bit of Bavaria
Pages 113, 121: © Dominic Bonuccelli

Salzburg, Austria
Pages 133, 156 right: © Dominic Bonuccelli

Practicalities
Pages 168 left, 175 left, 177 left: © Dominic Bonuccelli

Additional images by Rick Steves, Patricia Feaster, Cameron Hewitt, Gene Openshaw, Ragen Van Sewell, Robin Stencil, Gretchen Strauch, commons.wikimedia.org

Unless otherwise noted, copyrights apply to photographs of artwork.

Avalon Travel
An imprint of Perseus Books
A Hachette Book Group company
1700 Fourth Street
Berkeley, CA 94710

Printed in China by RR Donnelley
Fifth printing July 2018.
ISBN 978-1-63121-078-5
ISSN 2377-6080

For the latest on Rick's lectures, guidebooks, tours, public radio show, and public television series, contact Rick Steves' Europe, 130 Fourth Avenue North, Edmonds, WA 98020, tel. 425/771-8303, www.ricksteves.com, or rick@ricksteves.com.

Rick Steves' Europe
Managing Editor: Risa Laib
Editorial & Production Manager: Jennifer Madison Davis
Editors: Glenn Eriksen, Tom Griffin, Cameron Hewitt, Suzanne Kotz, Cathy Lu, Carrie Shepherd
Editorial & Production Assistant: Jessica Shaw
Researchers: Gene Openshaw, Ian Watson, Gretchen Strauch
Maps & Graphics: David C. Hoerlein, Sandra Hundacker, Lauren Mills, Mary Rostad

Avalon Travel
Senior Editor and Series Manager: Madhu Prasher
Editor: Jamie Andrade
Associate Editor: Maggie Ryan
Copy Editor: Denise Silva
Proofreader: Kelly Lydick
Indexer: Stephen Callahan
Production & Typesetting: McGuire Barber Design
Cover Design: Kimberly Glyder Design
Interior Design: Darren Alessi
Maps & Graphics: Kat Bennett, Mike Morgenfeld, Brice Ticen

ABOUT THE AUTHORS

Rick Steves

Since 1973, Rick has spent about four months a year exploring Europe. His mission: to empower Americans to have European trips that are fun, affordable, and culturally broadening. Rick produces a best-selling guidebook series, a public television series, and a public radio show, and organizes small-group tours that take over 20,000 travelers to Europe annually. He does all of this with the help of a hardworking, well-traveled staff of 100 at Rick Steves' Europe in Edmonds, Washington, near Seattle. When not on the road, Rick is active in his church and with advocacy groups focused on economic justice, drug policy reform, and ending hunger. To recharge, Rick plays piano, relaxes at his family cabin in the Cascade Mountains, and spends time with his partner Trish, son Andy, and daughter Jackie. Find out more about Rick at www.ricksteves.com and on Facebook.

Gene Openshaw

Gene has co-authored a dozen *Rick Steves* books, specializing in writing walks and tours of Europe's cities, museums, and cultural sights. He also contributes to Rick's public television series, produces tours for Rick Steves Audio Europe, and is a regular guest on Rick's public radio show. Outside of the travel world, Gene has co-authored *The Seattle Joke Book.* As a composer, Gene has written a full-length opera called *Matter* (soundtrack available on Amazon), a violin sonata, and dozens of songs. He lives near Seattle with his daughter, enjoys giving presentations on art and history, and roots for the Mariners in good times and bad.

FOLDOUT COLOR MAP

The foldout map on the opposite page includes:
• Maps of Munich on one side
• Maps of Munich Transportation, Bavaria & Tirol, King's Castle Area and Salzburg on the other side